Disclaimer

The contents of this book are for informational and *educational* purposes only. The information presented may contain sensitive, controversial topics relating to secret military programs, neuroweapons, targeted individuals, black magic, and satellite technologies. While every effort has been made to ensure the accuracy and reliability of the information provided, the authors do not claim to have direct access to all details or the full scope of the topics discussed. Some information has been taken from public sources.

Some aspects of the book's content may be speculative or taken from unconventional sources, and the reader is advised to approach the material with critical thinking and discernment. The authors and publishers are not responsible for any consequences that may arise from the interpretation or use of the information in this book.

The presentation of military and *covert* activities, and any reference to practices such as black magic, is intended for illustrative purposes and does not imply endorsement or encouragement of such actions. This book does not promote illegal, immoral or harmful behavior and should not be used as a guide to such activities.

All rights to information belonging to other authors are entirely theirs. It is futile to search for certain information online. It disappeared before the book was published. Some may have been re-uploaded. The reasons are self-evident.

The book although redacted numerous times *was found* with typos and more. This is not the first time that the content has been interfered with. Thus, with all due care and respect to the reader, it should be pointed out that where *anomalies* of expression and/or wording, typographical, should be found they should be ignored and not considered as lack of care and/or respect. The targeted individuals already know that these practices are common to the detractors who target them.

By reading further, the reader recognizes and understands the sensitive nature of the topics covered and takes full responsibility for his/her own interpretation and use of the material presented. God help us all!

I had a destiny and a destination
I've still have it and I'm going towards it.
Everyone has a purpose.
Mine was to publicize an ancient method.
Ours was to publish this book.
Prima materia
Codex 11,11
Codex 9.9

The Program

"All that is necessary for evil to flourish is for good people to do nothing. And that is exactly what is happening today. People who cry out to family members and friends, to local law enforcement and the FBI, to their government, to the military, to the private corporations that are involved in this, are met with silence or even worse, ridicule. They are accused of being crazy. They are accused of being paranoid and schizophrenic. And, as I will detail, mental health organizations are complicit in this by making false diagnoses.

Under full cover of what is in fact a social engineering program and a secret research and development program for some of the most sophisticated and advanced technology the world has ever seen. " **Brian Kofron, former SIS agent** .[1]

"This disturbing message is for the several million Americans and anyone else who cares deeply about the future of their country and planet Earth. The United States is in grave danger. Strangely, the danger comes not from

---

[1] Bryan Kofron (Justin Carter), whistleblower, former security expert at SIS/Security International Systems Inc, a private security firm in Seattle, Washington

foreign enemies, but from domestic enemies. The United States and most of the Western world are ultimately controlled by an unelected and irresponsible cabal." **Raul Hellyer, Former Defense Minister-Canada**

"At its apex is the banking and finance cartel, followed by the oil cartel, the CEOs of the largest and most powerful transnational corporations, the major intelligence agencies, including the CIA, FBI and NSA, and a significant part of the US military. Their collective power and influence is incalculable.

And their plan for the US, and for all of us, is alarming: automated computers, the programmed software of supercomputers will manipulate the emotions, behavior, and thoughts of everyone in the United States. It is horrible. It is horrifying. And it is a crime against humanity.

This is something that needs to be addressed immediately by lawyers and civil rights advocates. We need laws right now to stop this because it has gotten out of control and it is getting worse. It's a system that has mobilized huge human and material resources to build a tightly knit, highly efficient machine that combines military, diplomatic, informational, economic, scientific and political operations.

I know for a fact because I was an insider and I've been part of this program and I've seen it work day in and day out. I am aware that there are entire cities in America now that are nothing more than a massive experiment in social engineering. Because all over the world we are opposed by a monolithic and ruthless conspiracy, which is based primarily:

- on conspiratorial means to expand its sphere influence
- on infiltration instead of invasion
- on subversion instead of elections
- on intimidation instead of free choice
- on guerrillas by night instead of armies by day.

What these people have done is turn this technology into a video game, and that's exactly how they approach it. They're approaching it as if they're playing on their computer a cross between Sid Meier's Civilization and Sims, where they control the whole civilization and they also control people on an individual level.

The overall effect of this technology is one that can control the state of mind, attitudes, thoughts, feelings, emotions and therefore motivations and subsequently the actions of the person concerned. All day, every day, 24 hours a day, 7 days a week, 365 days a year.

It is an extremely sophisticated technology. It's one that produces total and complete mind control over the person. And it is now in the hands of people who are using it for nefarious purposes, for extremely evil and destructive purposes against individuals like myself. I am now an **individual targeted** by this technology because I have decided to speak out about it. Its preparations are hidden, not publicized. Its mistakes are buried. No expense (regarding the weapon) is questioned, no secret is revealed. I was told not to reveal anything, being threatened in various ways. That's why, before going public, I reported all of this four times to the FBI. I reported all of this to local and state police. I reported all of this to everyone and anyone I could. I tried to warn the company I worked for and the federal government of the United States of America. Unfortunately, I was confirmed that I am **not** crazy, and I was not told *we have no idea what you are talking about*, but I was told, by the Federal Bureau of Investigation and the Tempe Police Department, that *what you are describing is a federal program. We know exactly what it is and therefore there is absolutely nothing we can do about it.*

It is obvious that, in this day and age, no American citizen can come forward to denounce a highly illegal and unconstitutional program that is being used to torture the American people every day. I am sorry, but this is unacceptable. It is your duty to protect the American people. It is your duty to investigate the serious crimes and misdemeanors that have been committed by the people entrusted with the preservation of this country, our Constitution and the American people. Unfortunately, what is happening in America today is that all of the people who were charged with protecting us *are asleep* at the wheel.

They have broken their oath and, either by complicity or complacency, are making or allowing this nightmare to take place on American soil. This social engineering program experiments on Seattle's homeless and general population using what most people are familiar with as *voice to skull* technology (synthetic telepathy).

However, this technology is infinitely more advanced than most people know. It can be used to completely control the thoughts and emotions of the person concerned and can therefore be used to control their actions. This program is illegal, unconstitutional and absolutely terrifying. Because this technology could be used against tens to hundreds of millions of Americans every day.

It can literally stop your own thoughts and replace them with other thoughts by sending thoughts into your head. And it's so sophisticated that you can't tell where these thoughts are coming from, there's no way to discern that they're coming from anywhere other than your own mind.

So you can imagine how bad it would be for people who don't even know this technology exists. And have these thoughts that they think are spontaneous. And that's exactly what it can be used for. It can be used to influence people's opinion, to get them to agree with a certain program.

It can be used to turn groups of people or individuals against each other. But if we consider this use and the fact that it is being used to alter emotions, thinking, and behavior, then we could consider the many, many millions of people across the country who are under the influence of technology today, right now.

Many of the subjects who are currently homeless because of this program were originally highly educated, successful people. Their lives are being systematically destroyed by this program, which uses *voice to skull* technology, organized harassment, career sabotage, and an intense *character assassination* effort that isolates them from society, leaves them unemployed, and turns family and friends against them.

It is an extremely illegal program. It is abused by people who have no respect for these subjects, for the welfare of those people who are being experimented on. They are evil in a way that I cannot understand and do not want to understand. The differences of opinion that I had with them after I became aware of the full extent of this program caused me to object, confront them, and eventually quit my job because of it.

As a result, I too became a target of this program. Now, every day, it's in my head: *You're the lab rat now, you son of a bitch. Don't you ever mess with us and don't dare even think about talking about it, or we'll kill you.*

If you're a target person, I know how difficult your life is, because I'm one too. And I want to personally apologize for the role I played in this program as an employee of *SIS Security Industry Specialists* in Seattle, Washington. What I did, and what my company did, and still does.

What the Amazon corporation is doing and what everyone I'm going to name in this podcast is doing is unacceptable, it's illegal, and it needs to be stopped immediately. If you're being tortured every day and every night, if you're unhappy because of what these people are doing to you through *Voice to Skull* technology, emotion manipulation technology, I want you to know that you are not alone.

There are millions of Americans in this country crying out for help. From their neighbors, from their family, from their friends, from their co-workers, and they are met with a wall of silence and confusion because the general public is simply not educated enough on the subject to be able to offer any real help.

Also, the people who run this program are the most powerful people in this country and therefore anyone like me who tries to take action against them will have the fight of their life. In this context of research and development, I have discovered that there is an application of *voice to skull* (V2K) technology that is known as **HiveMind/HiveMind or Hive Group**.

It is now many, many hundreds of years more advanced than what people are generally aware of. And for the targeted person who is isolated, you can understand what a nightmare this is, because the complementary organized stalking program isolates her from everyone else in her community and she has nowhere to turn for help.

I do this for the victims. It's for the people who are alone and scared and being tortured by their government every day. I knew that once I decided to go public, the most powerful people in this country would be angry with me. And they are.

Since I uploaded my first podcast, I've been harassed nonstop. There has been a tenfold increase in the disgusting attitude I deal with from people who are assigned to harass me in groups. They have also threatened my life. I have obviously annoyed the wrong people.

What these people have done is turn this technology into a video game, and that's exactly how they approach it. They're approaching it as if they're playing a cross between Sid Meier's civilization and Sims on the computer, where they control the whole civilization and they also control people on an individual level. The overall effect of this technology is one that can control the target's mood, attitudes, thoughts, feelings, emotions, and thus motivations and then actions all day, every day, 24 hours a day, seven days a week, 365 days a year. This is extremely sophisticated technology. It is one that produces total and complete mind control over the target.

And it is right now in the hands of people who are using it for nefarious purposes, for extremely evil and destructive purposes against individuals like myself. Now I'm a target of this technology, because I've decided to talk about it, to try to shed some light on it, and to try to make some progress. *The test subjects-the people* being experimented on, or *the targets,* as they are called in the program, have already learned, that one of the key ways to cover up this program is to use the profession of psychology to do so.

If test subjects, the targets, talk about this problem they are referred to psychiatrists. This is to be evaluated and given diagnoses of schizophrenia, multiple personality disorder, delusions, paranoia, depression, so that they are discredited. So if they continue to speak out, or if they start to have any progress against this program, they will be inherently discredited. Because those who run this program will simply publish the psychological records and claim that the person is mentally ill.

This is a perfect way to cover such a technology whose main, and most popular, most well-known feature is voice to skull, which induces sound into the cranial cavity of the test subject, the target itself, so that when that person talks about it, when they seek help from their peers they will ask:

What's the matter with you, and the target will say: *I hear voices.*

In my mind, obviously, if members of the general public are not aware of the existence of this technology, and many of them are not, then they will interpret this as worrying. They will feel worried for the target and conclude that this person must be crazy. As result, they will recommend a psychological evaluation for the person.

You can see how this is going to play out. And so it is now, as good people, helpless people who are abused, tortured, enslaved, and experimented on in today's America, American citizens *(and beyond)*, cry out for help from fellow Americans, and fellow Americans respond:

Why don't you take some Prozac? Because we think you're schizophrenic.

Well, this is a highly technical program. All symptoms are induced by a technology that is so sophisticated, it's horrifying beyond description. This technology can be used to *teleport* images and even movies into one's brain. Static images and moving images that are so realistic that you feel like you are watching a movie or seeing something in real life.

It is like a 3D virtual reality rendering that takes place in the target's mind. This technology can also be used to control the target's muscle movement. It can take control of someone's hands or feet while driving and make you hit the accelerator or brake. This can be used to cause accidents.

It can also be used to prevent accidents from happening. This technology can also access the target's optic nerve and auditory system, so that those monitoring the target can see what they see and hear what they hear. This information is then downloaded and stored on a computer in a classified, highly secure location on servers that are guarded by one of the strictest security measures in the world. So the individual's entire day, everything they see, everything they hear, everything they experience and everything they feel is recorded until the end of time. This technology can also be used to manipulate the emotions of the person concerned. It can induce fear, love, hate.

It can make you nervous. It can make you confident. It can make you depressed. It can make you happy. It can make you feel any damn emotion at any time by artificially inducing them. This technology can also be used to induce and control dreams.

It can be used to control dream cycles and sleep patterns. To make you sleep very deeply or not sleep at all. This technology can also be used to mimic spiritual experiences. Joy, love, peace beyond all comprehension can be artificially induced by this technology to make the target believe they are having a genuine spiritual experience when they are not. This technology can also be used to read the target person's thoughts verbatim. As they appear in your own mind. This technology is so advanced and so sensitive that it can literally make you feel attracted to another human being. And make another human being attracted to you. And in doing so, they play the role of matchmaker.

They play Cupid and actually unite couples and make them fall in love. They also do the opposite. They also break couples apart. They break up families, husbands and wives. They separate children from their parents. They break up businesses and corporations.

They use this to manipulate society at all levels for their own benefit and gain, and they do so with an attitude of utter immaturity and, for want of a better word, utter malice. It is infuriating, it is very, very illegal and it must be stopped now. They see this as a massive game and a massive joke they are playing on the American target and the American people *(the world)*.

It is horrible. It is appalling. And it's a crime against humanity. It is something to be dealt with under the Geneva Convention. It is something that needs to be dealt with in international courts. This is something that needs to be addressed primarily by the Supreme Court of the United States.

This needs to be addressed until we get to that point, both at the local and state level. It is something that needs to be addressed immediately by lawyers and civil rights advocates. We need laws right now to stop this because it has gotten out of control and is getting worse.

The entire population of the United States of America could one day be controlled by this system. This is not a good thing. It is something that just messes with people and makes their lives a little more uncomfortable. It is something that has serious long-term psychological effects on the target. It is something that causes serious long-term physical damage to the target.

They are bombarded 24 hours a day, 7 days a week with radio frequency, microwave signals that literally *fry* their bodies. Every day and every night. And as a result, they age at an accelerated rate. Their lives are brought to a premature end.

This technology radiates teeth directly into people's mouths. This technology damages the individual's muscles. This technology damages the joints and the bones of the targeted individual to a point where if they have been under the influence of this technology for many, many, many years, the long term effects of this technology is that it will leave them completely disabled.

There are places where you can see the long-term effects this technology is having on people. In homeless shelters in Seattle, Washington.

So, if you are someone who is part of this program and you know that every word I say is absolutely true, please, get off your ass and do something about it. Stop agreeing with it. Speak up, blow the whistle, go to the authorities, report it. All of you who can do it, go to Congress, go to your congressman, go to your senators, go to your local law enforcement, go to your neighbors, go to your family, go to your friends, spread this news around the world so that we can ease the suffering of these innocent victims, targeted individuals who get this shit beamed into their heads every fucking day and somehow manage to survive and endure.

I want to thank you for hanging in there. You are my heroes. You are the reason I keep going forward every day. You are the reason I haven't given up. And you are the reason I'm talking about this now. As an industry insider and someone who has all the knowledge of how this program works. I felt a responsibility to speak out to help people like you because my heart goes out to you every time I see you post something online.

And I know there are millions of other people who have failed to post anything online. And I want you to know that I support you, we all support you, and we have to get through this together. But one of the things that worries me is that the technology that's being researched and developed in Seattle, using emotion manipulation and behavior manipulation, without the game starting and without the *voice-to-skull/V2K* program features

Thus, this use of technology can be done very discreetly, to the point where the person against whom it is being used will not know that the technology is being used against them.

And this is one of my main concerns and one of the reasons why I want to shed more light on this technology and this issue, because this technology could be used against tens to hundreds of millions of Americans every day. Because instead of using it, as most people believe, only against the individual, the targeted individual, this technology is only being used against entire populations.

From small groups of people, 10-20-100, to medium-sized groups of people, a few thousand to tens of thousands. This is done by creating a field effect, or a whole field of electromagnetic energy. It is created in a geographic location and any human being in that geographic location, within the electromagnetic field that resides in that geographic location, will be affected by the technology.

It can be used to induce a general mood in a population or crowd of people. It can be used to make them passive. It can be used to make them agitated. And it can be used to provoke or stop induced riots. *Stop the killing, start the killing. Stop the thinking, start the thinking.* Massive citywide mind control.

And I know for a fact, having been a connoisseur of this program, having actually been a part of it and seen it work day in and day out, that there are now entire cities in America that are nothing more much than a massive experiment in social engineering. There are field effects where this technology is not directed at an individual, but creates a general field of frequency in a geographic area so that everyone in that geographic area feels the effects of the technology.

It's more a general application of technology than a specific individual application of technology. I've seen it done and it's remarkable how effective it is, because you walk down a street in Seattle and you literally see sum all the people are in a bad mood, all at the same time, and they don't know each other. And then you go over a block or two, to a different office building, and exactly the same thing happens there.

It is very, very, very, very worrying. So inside that van, that general bubble or that general frequency zone where everybody, let's say, is in a bad mood, they can inject what would be an individual frequency specific to the targeted person. Let's say a homeless person in Seattle that they are experiencing 24 hours a day.

They will find themselves under the influence of the general state of agitation or bad mood that everyone else is in, and then they can be manipulated further by the frequency that is directed exclusively to them. Perhaps more than any other city, Seattle, Washington, seems to represent what America is becoming.

Amazon, Microsoft, Starbucks are all headquartered in the city or its suburbs. Jeff Bezos, the richest man in the world, lives there. But as well as unfathomable wealth, there is desperate poverty. And widespread decay. Homelessness in Seattle is on the rise. The city is suffocating under the garbage produced by hundreds of homeless encampments. Local news broadcasts recently held national headlines, warning that Seattle is dying. The city is becoming uninhabitable for ordinary families. Do you think drugs are one of the main drivers of homelessness? I think mental health is. Mental health is at the root, as you know, of a lot of addictions and other things.

Homelessness is complicated. Drugs are not the only cause. Take a look at this picture of people living in wrecked caravans. Starbucks world headquarters in the background. Like much of the West Coast, Seattle's economic boom has not been evenly distributed. Far from it. When wages at the lower end of the economic spectrum fail to keep up with the rising cost of living, you end up in a place where people living in cars are flanked by millionaires like Jeff Bezos and Bill Gates.

So, what causes homelessness? Everything that is done through this program is intended to have a psychological effect. And the psychological effect is meant to complement the effect that the technology has on the individual, so that they are brought to a point in their life where they are isolated, broke, unemployed, have no family, have no friends, and no one in the general public can detect or track anything that is being done to them, because the technology is used remotely and wirelessly and there are usually no physical signs left on the individual that anything is being done to them.

City elites have launched a coordinated information campaign aimed at voters frustrated with the official response to homelessness. Earlier this month, leaked documents revealed that a group of prominent nonprofits, the Bill and Melinda Gates Foundation, and the Campion Advocacy Group Fund, the Rakes Foundation, and the Ballmer Group had hired a public relations firm-Pyramid Communications-to conduct polls, create messaging, emulate the emotions, behavior, and thoughts of all people in the United States, all of which can be done remotely. It looks a lot like the New World Order tracking microchip, this whole control grid that is supposed to be implemented against the American people someday, and I'm here to tell you it's already here.

There will not come a day when there are troops on the streets and tanks *running* through your neighborhood and riot gear. We may have isolated incidents like that, and I've seen them from time to time.

The real control grid is this technology: *Voice to Skull, Hive Mind Behavior Manipulation Technology/* V2K, Behavioral Manipulation through group or hive mind manipulation.

And it can all be done remotely. It can be done by simply targeting you with frequency, by locking into the resonant frequency of your DNA and your mind. And in this way, track you, locate you and control you completely, 24 hours a day."[2]

All rights to this speech belong to **Bryan Kofron** former employee of Security International Systems Inc.

Cybertorture by states, corporate actors and organized criminals 2020

---

[2] The material can be found at the following address, if it is still available *Targeted Individuals Mind Control Mind Control Voice to Skull Electronic Harassment Gang Stalking* By A SIMULATED REALITY LIVINGSTONE, Publication date 2020-04-16 Topics Youtube, video, People & Blogs, Item Size 140156441/B. Kofron *Worked on Amazon's black projects in Seattle*

"**Nils Melzer**, professor of international law at the University of Glasgow and UN special rapporteur on torture and other cruel, inhuman or degrading treatment or punishment, warns that the internet could be used systematically to target individuals from afar - *through intimidation, harassment, surveillance, public shaming and defamation.* A staunch critic of the British government's failure to conduct an investigation into the rendition of jihadist suspects after September 11, Melzer also expressed concern about Britain's treatment of WikiLeaks founder Julian Assange in Belmarsh prison.

Later this month, the professor, who is Swiss, will present a report* to the UN Human Rights Council in Geneva, outlining his concern about the *continued growth of psychological torture and legal misconceptions about conduct prohibited by international treaty.*

[...] One alarming development Melzer considers is cyber-torture. States, corporate actors, and organized criminals, he says, *not only have the ability to conduct cyber operations that cause severe suffering to countless individuals, but may choose to do so for any of a number of torture purposes. Cyber-technology can also be used to cause or contribute to severe mental distress while avoiding physical bodily conduct, in particular through intimidation, harassment, surveillance, surveillance, public shaming and defamation, as well as the appropriation, deletion or manipulation of information.*

Harassment already in relatively limited environments can expose the targeted individuals to extremely high and prolonged levels of anxiety, stress, social isolation and depression, and significantly increases the risk of suicide. Therefore, it can be said that the much more systematic, government-sponsored threats and harassment conveyed through cyber-technologies not only involve a situation of actual powerlessness, but may well cause levels of anxiety, stress, shame and guilt that amount to severe mental distress, as is necessary for a finding of torture.[3]

---

[3]Source
https://www.researchgate.net/publication/351482707_Cybertorture_by_states_corporate
Report of the Special Rapporteur* Distr.: General, March 20, 2020. A/HRC/43/49. Available at: https://undocs.org/A/HRC/43/49 , accessed May 11, 2021. From: Bowcott, O. (2020)).
UN warns of rise of 'cyber-torture' to circumvent physical ban. The rapporteur warns against trivializing psychological torture as states exploit the internet to target individuals.
The Guardian February 21, at:
https://www.theguardian.com/law/2020/feb/21/un-rapporteur-warns-of-rise-of-cybertorture-to-bypass-physical-ban?CMP=Share_AndroidApp_Other , accessed May 11, 2021.
*Human Rights Council. Forty-third session. February 24-March 20, 2020. Agenda item 3. *Promotion and protection of all human rights, civil, political, economic, social and cultural rights, including the right to*

This book has an informative and sometimes narrative purpose. The authors of the book have experienced and lived the psychic torture described in the book.

Moreover, it is information (from various sources) documented and written by some of the authors, former agents who have personally experienced and seen this technology and related programs. These authors include: Brian Kofron (former SIS agent), Robert Duncan (former CIA, NSA agent, programmer), Daniel Estulin, Peter Levenda and others who have uploaded video and published written material.

The book is intended to help people, and to clarify, where necessary, the chaos, the traumatizing experiences, and give a possible explanation. Please do not panic, or think there is no support.

You will find extrapolated excerpts from books (because the subject is very well presented by the respective authors, no need for additions), public information that I have found in the course of personal research I have done to find out what happens to us, and to other people. The cited authors have done a very good job which is why I have included entire

---

development. Torture and other cruel, inhuman or degrading treatment or punishment

passages that reflect a reality that many live in silence. Data from past and present put together to create the big picture. Do not remain silent. All institutions/organizations with a military profile, and beyond, in all countries or any other private entities that develop such weapons, programs, devices should provide guarantees that the weapons, devices, are not being used non-consensually against the population, and be subject to rigorous vetting to ensure a protected environment for the people in all respects. Every institution and organization must be held accountable and checked. We need, and must have, such specialized and incorruptible organizations.

But this can be done if there is empirical data gathered from people with similar symptoms and the right actions are taken.

Some information has not been included and/or has been included without detail in order to protect readers.

After analyzing the available information, our conclusion is that no one is in absolute control, regardless of the type of weapons or methods of behavioral and mental manipulation developed, the existence of state secret departments, paranormal training bases and paranormal studies, advanced technologies, psychotronic weapons created, or technological, informational and psychological conflicts conducted. All these elements are subordinated to a higher will, a principle that was, is and will remain constant.

Of course, many organizations, regardless of their nature and their supporters, can cause considerable damage, but more often than not, these actions are countered by strong opposition from other entities, including the people, and not only.

In the meantime, cosmic phenomenology continues to deepen the mystery: either asteroids are approaching, satellites are being destroyed, or various secret bases are being affected by unexplained phenomena such as unidentified 'lightning bolts' or plasma activity in specific areas. In parallel, signals are being transmitted to Pluto by satellites of unknown origin that have been orbiting the Earth for hundreds of years, and some objects orbiting our planet are inaccessible to reconnaissance ships, which are destroyed when they approach them.

Thank the Good Lord it is so, and control can only be held by the Good Lord!

Even evil knows how much evil to do.

It knows where to stop because the universal equilibrium draws its limit. Only some creatures and technology don't know where to stop.

Any imbalance has its origin in a will external to the divine will.

Although our spiritual mission on Romanian soil ended in 2005, in 2014, through a forced intervention, we were called back to one of the most difficult missions we have ever had. We are writing to you here by the will of the Good God, the benevolent watchers and the invaluable help offered by certain truly benevolent people, perfected people, good, balanced teachers, from Romanian and foreign lands, families and many dear ones who helped and protected us. We felt the unconditional love, protection and guidance of all. They did it unconditionally only because it is their nature, their purpose and because they want the good of humanity, and for this we thank them completely. May the good God bless them, protect them and give them all that is best and beautiful, and in addition all that they desire, because they deserve it. We carry them in our hearts with great affection and love.

We write these lines for those who are going through or are about to go through an ugly and insidious reality. Mental torture and all that comes with what is included in the program.

We have been used in unspeakable and indescribable ways, so humiliating and degrading are the manipulative techniques to which the targeted individuals, predominantly those who oppose the oppression of the freedom we are born with, are *blindly* exposed. And we do not say this lightly. Psychic torture leaves no trace and usually comes *across* as part of some greater plan or initiation (not!). We personally have experienced a major regression, an attack on our own dignity; a battle of souls and brains, not an elevation, so it is safe to say that we have experienced hell. An inferno artificially and premeditatedly produced by other people, most likely people who have gone off the rails.

But we have known a dimension of the world that has been hidden for a long time, and this has been made possible by a cumulative effort, both physical and spiritual.

We hope that these lines will bring you a settling of thoughts and explanations that may be of help to you, so more clarity. For any further clarifications, healings or other enlightening information we invite you to seek out people who are trained to do so, genuinely good, good-hearted, not just pretending goodness.

If you feel that the lines you read here have a negative impact on you, don't read them at the time or put the book aside. Come back when you are stronger, or simply don't read it. And we don't say this lightly. That's why we've modified certain passages in the quoted texts and reworded them to remove the negative programming and despair that some of the posts insert.

Not because the cited authors wished to program negativity, but because the experiences are so negative, atrocious, and alter a being so much that it is very difficult for the person who has been subjected to this torture to write about it without referring to the negativity they have experienced.

There is a desperate attempt to erase memory, and going through the book you will read about the major interest that the German services, and not only the German services, have had in memory erasure in particular.

We did our best, and frankly it is a book written with many obstacles, mental attacks, obstacles, deviations and so on, many interferences, so written at a time when there were less electromagnetic emissions targeting us that *prevented* us from synthesizing information and so on. Not only did we not have access to many of the sites, access being blocked or restricted by external sources, but even buying some books was met with difficulties.

We have had times when we couldn't get out of bed and sit up, let alone take a shower. It took us a few years to get our strength back, and in the last few years we have actually fought for our rights. An invisible struggle that becomes visible in the sequences that materialize after the invisible struggles are over.

We have had to start over too many times and have had to overcome many obstacles put in our way even to find a job. We had our contacts wiped, stolen from our home, killed loved ones, pets, entered the house *in absentia*, placed various matters in food and drink, staged many injustices, constantly attacked by electromagnetic and other devices (so resented).

We have been stalked and harassed in ways so hard to explain and prove, with attempts to induce panic and paranoia, and all sorts of moods, direct and indirect threats Our phones, personal computers and those of our loved ones have been hacked, listened to, our personal gadgets have been hacked, too many times by losing all the data on them, our contacts, offers, conversations have disappeared, until, we believe, the detractors of the programs started to be hacked and listened to, until it started happening to all of them, right in their own *homes.*

They tried to destroy relationships with people dear to us, and they succeeded because we didn't know what we were dealing with. The technologies are manifold but in the book, you will find descriptions of some of the weapons, devices currently in use (or what is reported in some sources) or a combination of these and others that have been scientifically proven, patents on old and new technological innovations, methods of manipulating the mind and thus behavior.

The subject of cyber and psy-tech attacks involves advanced technologies and hacking techniques designed to affect both a person's physical and psychological security. In the following, we provide an overview of how these attacks can occur and who is usually behind them, based on available sources.

"How does cybercrime happen and who is behind these attacks?

Before executing a psychotronic attack, the killer

hacks the devices and different types of communication devices used by the target. This could include hacking cell phones, landlines, internet, e-mail, mail, Wi-Fi connections and security cameras. Electronic voices are then transmitted using microwaves or satellite. The criminal can be in a remote location or nearby using a computer.

Advanced forms of such an attack could also be the covert injection of neurotransmitter chips that are assigned cell numbers. These would run through the electricity of the targeted persons' bodies. These cell phone numbers are then run through a computer, that computer translating your thoughts. This technology has been available or supplied to the US military for sixty years.

US FFHS member Derrick Robinson says that, depending on the scale of the attacks, such mind games could be carried out by anyone, such as corrupt contractors, elements of a government, as well as private citizens. Thus, the perpetrators of these attacks could be an individual with a network of conspirators, a business or a corporation."[4]

---

[4] Ms. Shilpi Jain, Dr. Madhur Jain, Yuvah L Kumar, "V2K and Electronic Harassment: Psychotronic Cyber Crime Techniques", International Journal of Scientific Research in Computer Science, Engineering and Information Technology (IJSRCSEIT), ISSN: 2456-3307, Volume 9, Issue 2, pp.334-338, March-April-2023.
Available at doi: https:

Some sources claim that attackers may use microwaves or satellites to transmit electronic messages or voices, which are perceived by the victim as sound or mental voice. These attacks can take place from long distances, using devices that may be close to the victim.

The success rate of the various agent lies in the suppression of as many people as possible who have suffered in silence, unable to demonstrate the mental nightmare they have been through.

We've seen them all over the world. People who couldn't talk about their suffering because mental torture is invisible and there is rarely any evidence of it. Empirical data can be considered which consists of the spectrum of similar symptoms shared by all victims of this insidious tactic of manipulation and harassment, and other physical evidence that some have obtained from analysis, hidden camera footage, witnesses, etc.

In context, it should be noted that some sources claim that many of the *mental illnesses* have been introduced and endorsed by the APA/American Psychology Association, by employees of the same social engineering social machines with all its implications, they are under total dominium.

These *diseases* are the perfect cover to continue the unrestrained use of psychotronic weapons. It is an evil that does not care how much money you have, influence, connections, or whose son/daughter you are. It is an evil that has only one goal: total control. And there's more.

Soul and faith.

They feed on people's suffering and want to destroy any trace of their faith, goodness, virtues by exposing them to much evil. They want to *destroy* the connection with God either through evil, bigotry, or/and events in order to prove that there is no one to protect you. There is!

They can't stand the connection with God, faith.

*

Autonomous robots as weapons of mass destruction are illegal under three international treaties. According to sources, the United States has violated each of these treaties in the categories of the use of lethal automated killing machines, non-consensual experimentation on humans, and stealth directed energy weapon systems involving electromagnetic wave propagation and more.

On Russia's proposal to ban the use of directed energy weapons, weapons that can affect the psyche and well-being of a population, the only government that abstained from voting on the issue of banning the use of these weapons was the government of the United States of America. Weapons of mental torture have since been *remarketed* in English.

This war has subjugated people of extraordinary potential, extremely capable, lovers of beauty, good, God, honesty, honor, people who like to live in truth, freedom, peace, love, creativity and a just society.

We felt it was our duty to write and publish some notes of personal experiences, because we know that there are many silent victims who need confirmation, explanations, possible help on their way. And we know that what is presented here is not even *a sliver of* what exists. It is a personal perception.

If you know someone in such a situation please give them the book, it may help them. This is our intention, to help as best we can.

Iiris is a real person who has gone through terrible psychic ordeals and more. She was trained from childhood for what she would experience throughout her life. Some detractors are still trying to find out who she was trained by.

The good God has endowed her with the strength to overcome and heal from an she believes absolute evil. She's still a target. She was taken by surprise by events that only top-secret organizations know about. No, they are not talked about, and not even in the most elite circles. Only a few have access to this information. But there is help. There are unseen protectors watching over us. Guardians who watch over us so that we may fulfill what we have to fulfill. Good God be with us!

"If something is good, it is also divine. Strange as it may seem, this sums up my whole ethos. Nothing is more difficult than not deluding oneself." Ludwig Wittgenstein, Posthumous Notes 1914-1951

We hope not to deceive ourselves and others.

π

2016-Bucharest

Iiris was returning to the capital of Romania after a prolonged stay at a military base in the Middle East. The readjustment to the city's reality was jarring—like a sudden, forceful landing. She struggled to reintegrate, sensing a profound shift in the behavior of the people around her. It was as if something invisible had gripped them, casting the city in a general air of negativity, a heaviness that even the laughter of children could scarcely lift. She had temporarily moved to a neighborhood she despised, but at the time, she had no other choice. Only later would she uncover the unsettling truth: she had been subtly manipulated into making that decision.

One Sunday, Iiris decided to visit the newly opened park, taking advantage of the perfect weather to read a few lines from a book about the mysteries of the Bucegi mountains. She found an empty bench and settled into a quiet spot.

No sooner had she started reading than the familiar disturbance occurred. Within moments, the area around her filled with people—loud, boisterous, as if on cue. It felt as though they had all positioned themselves there deliberately, surrounding her in a purposeful, unsettling way.

Iiris chose to ignore the incident once more, convincing herself that it was nothing more than a series of coincidences. She continued reading quietly, focusing intently on the details in the book. She marveled at what she was discovering, wondering whether there was any truth behind the theories presented. She longed to see the artifacts and places described in the mountains of Romania with her own eyes.

Suddenly, she felt a subtle pull from her right. Her nerves picked up faint disturbances, but she dismissed them. With the chaos unfolding around her, she didn't want to let it distract her from her reading. However, the interference grew stronger, more insistent, and this time, irritation washed over her. She glanced ahead, then to her right. There was a man in the distance, his gaze carrying an unspoken message, but she quickly moved past him. Then, her attention shifted to an elderly man seated beside her. He had an imposing presence, exuding an air of respect and quiet authority. Iiris instinctively probed his energetic field, but found little to reveal.

He is a man trained in the field and seems to be from the system, she said to herself.

The field around him was protected as if by an outer shield. She didn't insist, and she didn't want to find out anything in particular about him, but she didn't understand why she had been insistently summoned. She put the book down and began to *listen to the subtle communication.*

She sat quietly, lost in her thoughts, oblivious to the noise and movement around her. Her gaze drifted to the small lake ahead, where children played along its edge. For a fleeting moment, a thought crept into her mind—one that stirred a feeling of regret, a sense of guilt for things left undone, as if the fault was her own.

She had been forcibly torn from her life in Romania, harassed throughout her studies and beyond. The constant upheaval had left her with no time to focus on her education, let alone attend classes. She had even been on the verge of giving up on her graduation exam. The pressure was suffocating, and it seemed as though there were forces determined to ruin her life.

At the time, she couldn't understand what was happening. For years, she believed it was just the way life unfolded. It wasn't until she looked back, analyzing the patterns over the past two decades, that the truth became clear. The same modus operandi, the same orchestrated attacks—she finally realized it wasn't just a series of unfortunate events, but a deliberate and coordinated effort, aimed at her and others like her.

These were issues that were far too much to bear for a woman who was taken so much each time, and all on her own hard work.

She came back immediately in present and turned her head suddenly toward the old man. She felt his pressure and looked at him, noticing how he kept his head bowed and his hand resting on the cane. He looked resigned.

After analyzing his features, his nonverbal language, *she listened* further. Iiris felt an anger that was not natural to her, and despite her best efforts at the time she could not decipher its origin, but she guessed it was from what the Elder had *said.*

Iiris stood up abruptly and left. She was feeling too much energy interference. She was very sensitive to the waves emitted and directed at her. At that time, she couldn't be around too many people for too long. She expected the old man to telepathically *say* something, but he didn't. At least this is what she thought at the time.

When he saw *la papesse* leave, he lowered his head. The woman felt a little guilty, but because she didn't fully understand what was going on, she chose to leave, telling herself that it was all in her imagination. She sensed that they were being monitored by other pernicious forces, both of them.

Iiris had learned that in certain circles she was recognized as *la papesse* and was considered equal to those of *the ecclesia*, though she could not even conceive of any association with any guild or organization. Those guilds killed her father on a sacrifice date specific to the same *modus operandi*.

Serving God was important to Iiris.

Him she loved.

As she passed the bench where the elderly man was sitting, he deciphered, "The frequencies have been sold!"

Iiris frowned and wondered to herself what this meant.

"What does this mean? Ah I'll stop worrying, when the time comes, if I have to, I'll know."

She headed to another place, quiet with only two people present in the area, a shady spot and only good for reading. Suddenly people began to pass by, who, as if on command, were saying certain words in tune and looking at her with intent. Four elderly ladies asked her permission to sit on the bench next to her.

"This is a public place. You don't have to ask my permission. And then you have two other benches you can use," Iiris said pointing to the benches in front of them.

"Yes, but we want to sit next to you."

"But why? Is there something special about this bench? I ask out of curiosity. I'd like to know the reason of your choice," Iiris asked visibly irritated and slightly ironic, recognizing the same subtle modus operandi she was already so familiar with. She got no answer, as was obviously to be expected.

Iiris realized that the scene was being repeated but with different actors, and decided to observe the methods applied. She pretended to read and audibly followed all the actions around her. She concentrated to note method and motive. She could not conceive this *taken by surprise*. There had to be a reason. But surely whoever was orchestrating this whole anomaly was trying to fake something, to induce some form of paranoia, possibly fear, and she knew she disliked being taken by surprise. So, someone who had studied her before. She was analyzing the symptoms in her field and in her body. She had her body on high alert, she could feel something acting from the outside, something creating stress and acidity in her body. She knew her body well, and the symptoms she had in different circumstances. It definitely wasn't organic, natural. She analyzed further.

Young men passing by her were repetitively and in chorus, as if at an unspoken command, uttering a certain word that seemed to be the key, which to her knowledge was supposed to trigger something at that moment, or later. She observed her mental and physical reactions and made some mental notes.

Three such groups passed. They all made intentional eye contact and they all uttered the same thing, in the same tone and exactly as they passed her, with a smile twitched in the corner of their mouths, as if it was a tape that scrolled in the same way. The volume and voice modulation were the same. She felt gusts of malice, negative energy, and wondered how they were being transmitted, because these young men didn't know her, and she didn't know them. She had never met or seen them before. She had an excellent memory, so at least a few and she would remember them. It seemed organized. There were patterns, precise patterns of behavior.

What about negative energy? Why negative energy? What have we done to them? And then what about this word? And so much hype about it, she wondered thoughtfully.

Interesting. Like they're being controlled to behave the same way. How bizarre. How do they do that? It's as if someone turns the volume up louder and slower as they please!" she remarked to herself and made another mental note to review later.

The elderly ladies laughed continuously as if on command the entire time they sat on the bench. However infectious and heartwarming the laughter, it sounded artificial and tiresome. They glanced at her now and then. Iiris perceived them out of the corner of his eye, but ignored them. They had left a few minutes after being ignored. She had noticed that in the meantime, on another bench, an unassuming old man had taken a seat, frail, but with a beneficent, reassuring presence.

All the years of observing human nature and the various inter-human, social, economic dynamics, the studies and books he had read, the background training allowed her to distribute his attention to external circumstances easily and to analyze verbal and non-verbal behaviors and the messages subtly transmitted, as well as the causes that generate such behaviors.

She briefly recalled one of the many episodes when she had been taught to observe how people choose to play different roles and alter the same reality according to the people in front of them. That is, to distort reality and themselves according to circumstances and presences.

She could inherently perceive the dynamics, and whether they were aimed at her or just random circumstances. It was those little details that marked the differences in substance. The old man who had remained on the bench where he had sat earlier, observed the scenes unfolding around Iiris. Eventually the place quieted down, but Iiris was in an inexplicably anxious state. She felt prickling in his tissues and had a discomfort she could not explain.

She closed the book and scanned the events to remember the details for later reflection. The old man then looked at her and said:

"Congratulations on reading! It's a rarity these days."

Iiris understood that the old man was referring to the details in the book and her on own personal research. Yet his words carried a deeper, more veiled meaning. It is the custom of those trained in the field to speak in a veiled and coded sense, letting the other information filter through the words.

From time to time, she used her skills to find out things hidden from ordinary people. She would link to the information in the book and author to determine how true what was presented was, and then visit the place presented and get further details through physical evidence. Sort of like remote viewing. She did remote viewing so often and for so long, and naturally, that until recently she was convinced that everyone did it. And maybe most did.

She stood up and left after the elderly gentleman had dissapeared without a plausible explanation. She gave him a moment to slip away quietly, resisting the urge to follow his movements with her gaze. However, after a brief pause, she glanced up to see which direction he had taken. The alley ahead of him offered only one way forward, while the street could be accessed either left or right from the sidewalk. The fence provided some visibility, yet it struck her as odd that he was nowhere to be seen within a 20-30 meter radius.

He was moving too slowly to have simply disappeared. It was as though he had vanished into thin air. This wasn't the first time she had witnessed someone inexplicably disappear from her sight.

She arrived home, determined to continue reading and after a short evening routine, she lay comfortably on her bed to savor her favorite type of reading. As soon as she read the first paragraph, she heard the words she was reading echoing, as if they were being read somewhere in her head, as if she was reading aloud to herself in her head. She quickly self-analyzed and turned off that effect that she didn't know. Then she heard a signal like a radio signal amplified and a sound as if a microphone had opened:

"What's up Iiris, can't you read?" asked the voice of an amused, ironic and arrogant man.

La papesse listened intently, and as she prepared to send him back to *his origins*, she sensed *a bios of* someone else, subtly conveying to her the subtle message to let him speak and not answer. All she could grasp was that there were two *energies,* one meant to be beneficial, the other evil. She sat and incredulously analyzed the whole scene, she knew it wasn't her thoughts, the intercept was clear, the artificial tinnitus effect came and went, so it was something on the radio or microwave waves.

She didn't know how she got into this whole telepathic charade, staged or not. She had been silently observing everything that had been happening to her and the way she had changed since she had returned to the country. She knew, she felt that she was not herself and was always striving to return to the potential she knew. That potential that involves having your soul in you, with you and at you.

Iiris would have monologues with herself when she wanted to figure something out, like math calculations with difficult equations, but she never had an interlocutor.

Having training from experiences that were extremely painful for her, a father who died in the system and a military brother who got indicted on a forged file, a mother who fought like a lioness after her father's death to provide her two children with at least a loaf of bread on certain days, some relatives through other institutions and other people she met *by accident* who were part of different institutions and organizations, she thought she was under some form of verification, especially since she had returned from the Orient base after a long stay. But that spontaneous dialog, and connected with the events in the park and with her work, showed that people were informed about what she was doing at the time, so she was being monitored in real time.

But why? How exactly? What was the reason? Out of the blue and for no reason?

Her family had been under scrutiny since she was a child; then her monitoring continued through college and subtly while she was away. Her father, as a child, always warned her not to answer the phone if it rang and not to give details of what was being talked about in the house, by name. He forbade her to say anything especially after he fell ill before he died.

Iiris never suspected that it was more than secretive matters of business. But it was about her. And her father defended her. She had no details, and when she was a teenager, she only wanted to get into a certain institution so she could have access to her father's file. She knew there was more. But she never accepted the offer she later received after college graduation because it meant betraying her family.

Iiris assumed that she was being monitored for her ability to decrypt informational algorithms and analyze them, but she didn't rule out some kind of verification for who knows what reason. Either way she was left with the impression that someone wanted to show her, prove something, and even induce *something* but she didn't know what was it. *Some kind of grand entrance! Pfff! That's how they like to make themselves known!*

π

The frequencies have been sold.

The microchip and the software which

controls people's minds.

He who has the bride is the groom.

The Second Prince.

The Son of Man will return as

The Second Prince

When the time comes, the stars will align,

A Poet Prince will be born from a Poet Prince

and will become once again

King of Kings.

Target individuals-as seen in the program

"As far as I know, the number of SIS[5] employees who have been subjected to the program's experiments is in the dozens, around twenty-four to thirty-six. That is all I know directly. And then, nationally *(in America)*, the estimates in terms of target individuals who still retain some sort of autonomy and freedom, and who have not been brought to the level of those in Seattle, completely enslaved by this program, would be estimated at a million-two million at this point in time and we're talking about target individuals who are exposed to this technology and are being watched 24/7. They are selected for many different reasons. Often because they are isolated. They don't have much money, friends or family. And they also tend to be very, very smart people. The aspects of this technology that they're interested in improving have to do with cognitive processes, with processing information. As a result, they want very smart people to be the targets of this program.

---

[5] **SIS**: In this context, this acronym refers to the *Service Information Secretariat*, which is the intelligence agency of a state (in some countries, this type of agency is known by various names such as MI5 in the UK or CIA in the US). It collects and analyzes secret intelligence to protect national security.

They also tend to target people who are involved in what I would call alternative research, commonly called conspiracists, who disagree with the government, people who research things like 9/11. They're also interested in people who are involved in research about this technology. We've found that a high percentage of people who are targeted are people who are interested in or have information about very advanced technologies.

Usually these are related to directed energy weapons, and frequency weapons. Exactly the type of weapons we're talking about here, that are used in *voice to skull/synthetic telepathy induced by voice to skull technology*, and behavior modification, and many other aspects of this technology. Each individual fits the general profile I'm describing.

So they're very intelligent, and it's in their interest to be isolated by any means necessary. They normally have a kind of, what I would describe as a free mind.

There are people who are not part of the crowd, so to speak, in the way they think. You know, they're *outsiders* (the black *lions* of society), they're what the government would call dissidents, or revolutionaries, or people who may be a problem.

Some TI-trageted *individuals* have said that this type of profile, that all targeted individuals fall into, is characterized by empowered individuals, and I would certainly agree with that. But I can't talk about how they actually identify such a target individual.

I think the general profile that I'm describing and that fits the targets of this program is something that is generated at a high level within the program.

This is the federal government. We're talking at the highest levels of this social engineering program. We are scientists from across the country and around the world.

They look at someone's genetics.

It looks at someone's cognitive abilities.

He's looking at someone's genes.

He's looking at someone's DNA.

They look at people's social situation.

They look at people's careers.

I was very surprised that so many PhD students are actually the targets of this program. They are usually PhD students who have gone against the mainstream of academia, of what academia normally teaches, usually in the fields of science and technology.

And the reason is that the people running the program want to cover certain technologies and certain aspects of science that can lead to extraordinary discoveries. These higher levels of science and technology are the exclusive purview of the classified branches of our government and military, and as a result, it follows that the American people have no right to this information and it is in the national security interest of our country to keep it classified.

But once these people are selected, they will have an entire tracking band (transmission frequency) of the *voice to skull/voice to skull* program running against them. This is detailed in my article at the *157 Roy Street* section of my website.

They will organize planned harassment and stalking campaigns, run career sabotage programs against them to ruin their jobs. They will have character assassination campaigns run against them in their neighborhood. They will be isolated from family and friends as these people are turned against them.

And they will be isolated slowly. slowly, over time, using the technology itself. Many people get scared, understandably, when they don't know what it is at first. Many times, they end up going to the psychiatrist and, false diagnoses of manic-depressive schizophrenia, delusional hallucinations, delusional paranoia are written against these individuals and it turns out that it is a loophole in the law that is being used to take away people's constitutional rights.

Because once you are deemed mentally incompetent, i.e. unable to take care of yourself, i.e. depressed, delusional, paranoid, the state or federal government uses that as an excuse to come in and say they have to take care of you.

So, I warn all targeted individuals, please do not go to a psychiatrist and do not allow them to make a diagnosis against you, because this is a dirty trick they are using to take away the rights of people all over the country.

This is discussed very openly within the SIS and with some of the liaison contacts in the EESC[6] , Amazon, as well as with members of the military who are in a civilian capacity. One thing you have to understand is that in the security field, most of the people who work there are ex-military and ex intelligence people.

And many of them, in fact, are still active intelligence agents. And they've simply been reassigned to the internal service to work with a private security company, specifically for the

---

[6] **The EESC** European Economic and Social Committee provides a forum for representatives of different economic and social groups to advise the European institutions on economic and social legislation.

purpose of running this highly illegal program that's being run against TIs/target individuals everywhere, so, target individuals all the way, what I would call people who are under the total influence of voice to skull/ V2K technology.

[...] But one of the things that worries me is that the technology, as it is being researched and developed in Seattle, uses emotion manipulation and behavior manipulation, without the *harassment play* and without the V2K/voice-to-skull technology features.

Thus, this use of technology can be done very discreetly, to the point where the person against whom it is being used will not know that the technology is being used against them.

And this is one of my main concerns and one of the reasons why I want to bring more clarity to this technology and to this issue, because this technology could potentially be used against tens to hundreds of millions of Americans every day. I recognize that I've mentioned in some of my podcasts that there are field effects where this technology will not be directed at one person, but it will create a general field of frequency in a geographic area so that everyone in that geographic area will feel the effects of the technology. It is more a general application of the technology rather than an individual, specific application of the technology.

But if we consider that use and the fact that it's being used to alter emotions, thinking, and behavior, then we could be looking at many, many millions of people across the country who are under the influence of technology today, right now. So in that general field they can broadcast a frequency that affects the human beings in that frequency field and induce a general state of happiness or sadness, anger, agitation, tranquility, and in that way have a general effect on the city; I've seen this done and it's remarkable how effective it is, because if you walk down a street in Seattle, you'll see people in a bad mood, all at the same time and not knowing each other, and then you walk over a block or two to another office building and walk in and see exactly the same things happening there. It's very, very, very disturbing. So, within this bubble or frequency zones everybody, is let's say in a bad mood. And under these conditions you can still *inject* a frequency specific to the targeted individual, say, a homeless person in Seattle that they experience 24 hours a day.

So, they will be under the influence of the general state of agitation or bad mood that everyone else is in, and then under the influence of the specific frequency that is directed at them.

They can literally turn off your own thoughts and replace them with other thoughts *(in some cases they don't)*, sending thoughts into your head. And it's so sophisticated that you can't realize where these thoughts are coming from. There's no way to discern that they're coming from anywhere other than your mind.

So, you can imagine how bad it would be for people who don't even realize this technology exists. And they have these thoughts that they think are spontaneous because they are under the influence of this technology.

And being on both sides of this technology, I am amazed/dismayed at how it works.

And I know that the thoughts that I'm putting into your head are coming from exactly the same place in your mind that your own natural thoughts come from. So, if I didn't know that I was under the influence of this technology, then I would have no idea that someone was influencing my thoughts. And that's exactly what it could be used for.

It could be used to influence people's opinions, to get them to agree with a particular agenda. It could be used to turn groups of people or individuals against each other for any purpose. This affects the most intimate part of the human being. It's a huge, huge problem. And you can imagine the applications of this if somebody ever wanted to start a riot, if somebody ever wanted to increase the crime rate, and then of course, you know you can use it for exactly the same thing but the opposite. You can use it to lower the crime rate by making everybody passive. And this, too, could have bad applications. If you want people to be passive, not paying attention and not taking action, it could be used for that as well.

So, yes, my mind boggles at the possibilities in terms of using this device."

Bryan Kofron-former SIS employee

π

2009- New York

Iiris had come out of the famous lingerie shop because she felt a strange pressure. She had to get out of there immediately and she didn't know why. She had long ago learned to listen to her nervous system and she sensed something was wrong. She had gone out for a smoke after telling her coworkers that she didn't want to be in the store much longer and would like to go back to the hotel the company had provided for her stay of a few days. She saw a woman of African descent outside the store staring at her as if she wanted to tell her something. She had the feeling that time had dilated as the woman stared at her. Finally, she croaked a "You are beautiful. /You are beautiful."

Iiris wondered why the woman had made that statement because it seemed as if she didn't actually mean to tell her that. Intuitively she looked herself up and down as if she wanted to understand something. The woman continued to stare at her and then she telepathically heard "Run!".

A sense of danger clutched at her, and she couldn't understand why in the warm New York *pasture* that woman had come just as Iiris had exited the store to telepathically tell her *to run* away. She tended to ignore unless intuition informed her otherwise. But she didn't understand, she had no idea what was going on. She wanted to continue to smoke, but because of the state of alertness she was in, she had re-entered the store, found her coworkers, and informed them that she wanted to leave immediately.

She found an excuse for the sudden change of mood and shortly they left for the hotel. The next day she was out sightseeing with one of her coworkers to see the famous New York City skyline and other sights. At the crosswalk, she felt dizzy and almost lost control of her body.

She quickly notified her friend, and intuitively and immediately aligned her energy centers without knowing exactly what she was doing. The prayer to God left as if from deep within and without warning. Something was protecting her. Certain codes activated instantly without her having any information beforehand. She felt as if something wanted to extract the essence from her body, she felt as if she was losing her breath, her soul, and she didn't know what could cause it. She remained in control of herself and after a few moments she was able to recover, feeling her breath coming back.

*What was **that** strange sensation? She said looking around herself. Probably agoraphobia. But the curious thing is that I've been so many times in hyper-crowded areas with so many people and I've never had this perception, these symptoms.*

I fly miles off the ground every day and am almost always in airports. I should have felt the same way at least once.

Iiris probed her past states and found no feelings like before. There was no panic, only a sense of helplessness and alienation. Something in her system informed her that it wasn't just a false alarm.

*

Later she would learn of the experimental weapon of a deviant faction operating in America and beyond, and that of something that would, as some would say, cut and *shackle* souls, leaving people feeling empty, soulless, a kind of extraction, but not total. If the weapon failed, then the innocent victim was subjected to experimentation to *bring them to their knees* by other methods in order to keep them in continuous trauma. Continuous trauma causes *total submissiveness. But to whom?*

She couldn't explain that feeling in New York until she read about the weapon, which some sources call it S.A.T.A.N.,

Silent Assassination Through Adapting Networks, or according to speculation about directed energy weapons or advanced technologies, has other possible interpretations. But as these meanings are not officially confirmed, they can be considered hypotheses. The authors believe that there is a subliminal name association between this directed energy weapon (given that it was mentioned in the book published by an American), and a weapon of the so-called enemies of the Americans, precisely to create an unconscious and subliminal association to strategically position *the cat in the overseas backyard* and come out innocents out of it.

π

The Weapon

Dr. Robert Duncan asserts that the so-called S.A.T.A.N. weapon, can be classified as *worse than lethal* because it is a weapon of maximum pain and psychological torture that can keep the body alive during torture longer than traditional methods of torture.

Find out how it could be used below.

This *system* doesn't actually target body parts, but rather renders pain sequences in the brain to be experienced exactly like the real emotions. You can't reason with a machine, you can't submit, you can't surrender. It will torture the person as programmed but responds ONLY to commands.

According to R. Duncan the system and its subprograms have the following applications:

-personality simulations, also called personality simulations by the DoD-Department of Defense Department of Defense

-collection of pathological and sociopathic thoughts, selection of mental viruses

- selecting human scenarios to be applied to the victim, mind probing
- inducing pre-recorded pains from other people, from open-heart surgery to nausea and dizziness, headaches, menstrual pain and pins and needles
-induced emotional pain, such as depression and other extremely negative thoughts, can be induced using this system.

More abstractly, the weapon:

- induces pains of all kinds, it is an internment camp without walls that has distributed personalized-electronic wards and mental incapacity (mental prisons) forcing people to keep moving through pain stimuli
-makes a person *crazy* by changing the pattern of correlations through brain circuitry
- induces behaviors modification breaking of random Pavlov patterns and reassociations.

The overall S.A.T.A.N. system includes many sub-programs such as Elisa, ALICE and TAMI.

All these are artificial voice responses and amplifiers of negative messages to demoralize, create despair, disable and discredit. This operating system is scalable and automated.

It can change vocabulary sets based on reading the target's mood. This is the modern version of McGill University's brainwashing research by Dr. Ewen Cameron. He used to watch loop (repetitive) recordings of his subjects without their consent, research that was funded by the CIA to *erase their* souls and minds.

These were just some of the basic techniques and do not include rape simulation, humiliation techniques, threats, profanation, desecration, suffocation, torture, sleep deprivation, deprivation of any kind, isolation, electroshock etc., subliminal suggestion, neuro-linguistic programming, hypnosis, *psychic induction/psychic* driving[7], imaginary combat weapons.

Torture and/or mental attrition leads to the distortion of good behaviors so that harmful ones can be programmed in their place. This behavior modification to the point of death, along with remote controlled heart attacks, is *effectively winning the hearts and minds of* any population.

---

[7] ***psychic driving*** was a psychiatric procedure in the 1950s and 1960s in which patients were subjected to a continuously repeated audio message on tape to modify their behavior.

The authors know that there is also a system that does the reverse. That's why you may feel the beneficial interference *guiding you* up constructive paths.

Tanatologists have achieved the creation of correlation between lethality risk factor matrices that are added to the S.A.T.A.N. system.

Thanatology is used in the CIA and DoD for two reasons. They are interested in how to better kill and bring a detainee to the brink of death during interrogations. They research modern medical studies that are designed to save lives and then use them to destroy lives. A pernicious dichotomy of economics that we the people endure.

While there are many programs for fear factors, the most *important* is the silent mode of execution of the weapon, which includes secondary and tertiary stressors. Not all mind-control behavior modification experiments involve death. As argued earlier there are also beneficial somatic systems that do the reverse and protect people from this *false system*.

Duncan further describes the weapon. It doesn't get quieter and more diabolical than that.

This was the *perfect* weapon because it has:

-lethality and ability to question or program large-scale effects on populations or individuals

-silent, undetectable and untraceable, so the public won't react to it and it can be used in *plain sight* anywhere on Earth

-*better* than viral, biological, chemical or nuclear weapons because there are no residual contaminants and no damage to infrastructure.

Further refinement of the correlation matrices can be developed for personality, language and cultural factor segmentations. This weapon system is easily scalable, since **Gabriel**[8] is the global communication system.

$$\pi$$

---

[8] More about Gabriel can be found in Robert Duncan's book *Project: Soul Catcher*

2016 – Bucharest

Iiris felt her soul tear apart from the pain, her entire body pulsing with it her tissues being burned with an unbearable heat. It was three in the morning, and she was alone in the rented studio. The pain made it hard to breathe. She heard someone ask her:

"After all this pain, you still choose love?"

"Love, always love. Love and truth."

Another wave of excruciating pain struck her. Iiris curled into herself, clutching her chest and stomach with all her strength. She was on her knees, unable to stand, but not fully kneeling. She could feel the pleasure of the person torturing her as this pain was inflicted on her.

She couldn't stay on her feet. Gritting her teeth, she cried silently, trying to hold back the sobs of helplessness. She didn't understand what was happening to her, nor why this was being done.

But before she could think further, she felt a surge of energy rise from within her, powerful and sharp, the moment the wave of pain hit. She looked upward, as if trying to trace its path. She had reached another point of light. Dazed from the agony, she tried to make sense of what was going on.

She intercepted another bio-signature—another living being, observing the scene. She sensed good intentions, as though the individual was following the signal emitted from her, perhaps trying to understand something about it, or maybe trying to create the impression that this was the case. In any case, it didn't bode well. The pleasure-infused cruelty wasn't a good sign. Someone was torturing her for their own pleasure, aiming to break her Spirit. She intercepted the animalistic pulse.

These were the kinds of people who thrived on transgression, those who had so much they became bored of normal living.

Others had found ways to extract the soul and power from others, Iiris thought, as she curled up on the floor, face nearly touching the ground. Gathering her strength, she knew she was God's warrior. She straightened, centered herself, and rose to her feet.

"You will dearly pay for everything you've done to me and to others.

There's **something** human about this, fore even evil knows how much harm to inflict."

She knew she was innocent. Then, she sensed a presence—something watching her from above. She focused intently, analyzing what she was perceiving to determine whether it was a projection or if someone was following her from that direction through some kind of device. She had read about the possibility of adapting technology to human DNA through resonance—a form of entanglement, a symbiosis between devices and humans allowing the transportation of energetic and conscious forms to a desired location. This adaptation enabled a type of extracorporeal travel to a specific point. The transfer was conscious, and those with extrasensory abilities could intercept the direction from which they were being monitored. She knew about governments' interest in using psychics, especially in covert operations. Her thought drifted instantly to a group that operated in the *Holy Land.*

Iiris assessed the sensations in her body.

Pressure in her chest and stomach—soul, will, and personal power, she thought.

She laid down in the bathroom, the only place in the apartment with natural elements on the floor. She felt like a person who had been brutally beaten. Her body ached, her head throbbed, and her temples pulsed rhythmically. Her flesh burned with fever. She wanted to take a shower to wash away the disgusting feeling in her being, but she had no strength left. There would be a day when justice would be done. God is with us, and this suffering is not from God. God is in me, He protects me, and He gives me the strength to endure this experience.

Her mind flashed back to the previous day when she heard the sound from the military unit. There were sonic waves, barely audible, muffled sounds, and subtle pulses. She felt them strongly, considering the distance and the blocking buildings around her.

Could it have been an experiment conducted without the public's knowledge?

Then her mind shifted to a location near the military unit.

Had they buried something in the underground area?

Her mind shifted again to the freshly installed antennas on nearby buildings. She could *see* the rooftops and stopped at a specific point where about twenty antennas were clustered in the area.

Iiris tried to sleep, finally managing after an hour of intense pain. After many such nights, she managed to sleep, but not before feeling the presence and gaze of a man observing her symptoms.

"Go ... and take it...!" Iiris responded with the international gesture of *thanks*.

For a long time, she hadn't known how to curse, as there was no swearing in her home. But during her university years, she had *befriended* some locals in Bucharest who welcomed her and helped her *adjust*. She had never used *this skill*, but now for some reason she could not understand, it served her well. This time, it seemed effective because the presence had departed, though not before analyzing the reaction of 'the priestess'.

Her determination to keep fighting had been noted. She too had been watching and analyzing him. Iiris had deciphered the informational algorithms of many individuals and the spaces in which they communicated. They wanted to know where she got her information from, how she communicated, and whether someone was transmitting this information to her. They even tried entangling, attempting to connect someone to her mental field in real-time. They wanted to perceive what she perceived and vice versa. An instant exchange of information between two or more people. What one learns, the other learns. What one knows, the other knows.

Iiris had been under surveillance for a long time, but since 1999, it had become more apparent. The military environment she grew up in gave her an advantage that many didn't have in such situations. Her phone was tapped, she was followed to university, to clubs, on the street, and at home. A car was always parked in front of the apartment in Berceni where she had lived during university. There was a man who sat in the vehicle for hours in front of the building, and Iiris couldn't understand who would waste so much time or why, but she had no idea she was being monitored.

She was used to analysing such anomalies because her father, a military man, was constantly surveilled. But he had died in 1994 under strange circumstances, as his colleagues and friends had, so there seemed to be no reason for her to be followed anymore.

Iiris found herself once again in bizarre situations, and after careful analysis and much time spent gathering data, she concluded that the only reasons for her surveillance were her extrasensory abilities and the way she assembled details, her cerebral activity, emotional reactions, and the plasmatic activity in her environment.

She later realized that what was happening to her resembled an execution pattern, and it was a method of observing the plasmatic activity around her, a connection with that cloudy, plasmatic presence. She would later learn more details about soul extraction and the recording of electromagnetic activity from the body. This engineering was publicly discussed by the British since 1996. She would also learn how much these detractors had worked to sever her connection with God.

It seems that the U.S. military had (and probably still has) programs to track individuals with psychic/psionic abilities. These are people with extrasensory or paranormal powers, as they are commonly known. This explains the numerous secret and unclassified research efforts in the field.

The operator of the S.A.T.A.N. weapon program can induce sensations of burning, tissue cutting, stabbing, and pain throughout the body caused by invisible stimuli. These sensations are mainly induced by stimulating specific parts of the brain corresponding to the relevant organ(s), and they are perceived in specific locations on the victim's body, or in multiple locations simultaneously. Thus, the victim may feel a warming sensation in their head or experience pressure in certain areas of their head.

The pain experienced by the targeted individuals is indescribable—a true, silent, living torture that can't be put into words, a torture that often leaves no visible marks.

Why me? Why is this happening to me? What did I do to deserve this?

Experiments, money, control, and energy extracted from the sacred soul created by God. Tormented souls. Who would benefit from such things? Why? The answer lies with you.

*

The operator of the S.A.T.A.N. weapon program can select to induce the sensation of burning, cutting of tissue, stinging, induction of pain that is felt throughout the body being caused by invisible stimuli.

These sensations are induced mainly by stimulating parts of the brain corresponding to the organ(s) in question, and will be perceived in a particular place on the victim's body or in several places at once. So, the victim will experience a warming of the head, or feel pressure in certain areas of the head.

The S.A.T.A.N. Weapon and the *Vodoo Doll* program have no comparable experience when it comes to the physical pain felt by a target individual when they are used on them.

Usually strange, new and extremely painful sensations are directly induced.

The weapon and its related programs, as R. Duncan describes, are used in silent warfare, interrogations, and eugenics programs; it's difficult to call the current use *tacit warfare*, because the targets have no way of surrendering or even knowing they are part of a war.

"For this reason, several treaties prohibit the use of automatic weapons systems. Predator drones and unmanned airplanes have human controllers not being fully autonomous. This weapon can be used without human operators, making it illegal under the Geneva Conventions. Torture is also illegal, but some countries' governments only respect treaties when they are in their favor.

The automation and scalability of these torture programs has been the focus of the last few decades. The pain caused by other people's misfortunes is recorded and cataloged, and then played back to the target brain repeatedly. The torture programs will latch onto whatever technique causes the most pain and stress and continue to play back to the target these emotions, from physical to psychological, demeaning and threatening, with silent, repetitive and chaotic and/or sequential repetitive and/or sequential sound.

This weapon has taken the title of the "Great Satan" of the United States among Arab groups and other nations. Propaganda and disinformation tactics used within mass information systems have helped to prevent ordinary people from realizing or understanding this connection.

Robert Duncan likens this weapon to hellfire. A hellfire that comes in many forms of microwave emissions used for burning torture, lasers, friction, ultrasound, oxidation, viral or bacterial rashes, frostbite, chemical burns, etc.

These methods are used as *no-touch* torture, and is applied remotely to target individuals. These are people who have been previously stalked, harassed, mentally and physically assaulted in one way or another, emotionally traumatized in order to make them more susceptible to programming.

Sources talking about this weapon often imply similarities to HAARP (High-Frequency Active Auroral Research Program) technology, a research program that has been linked to speculation about weather manipulation, mind control or the transmission of targeted energy. However, there is no official evidence or confirmation to support the existence of this weapon in the form it is described.

The black ops through which such weapons would be operated are kept off the government's financial books and, for the most part, away from public scrutiny. In this context, shadow *government* is a term used for:

- to refer to the Department of Defense and security agencies that use covert technologies (to the detriment of a segment of the population) in their clandestine internal operations;

- referring to a government that would take over if Washington D.C. *falls.*

R. Duncan, *Project:Soul Catcher/Project:Soul Catcher*

Most of the communications infrastructure, with dozens of acres of computers, is housed in semi-secret underground bases in the US and allied territories. Semi-secret because the antenna fields are difficult to conceal as they are mostly above ground and occupy many kilometers.

The decision after the Geneva Conventions to ban autonomous robotic systems in warfare is based on the reasoning that the robot has no way of recognizing when someone surrenders. Similarly, in the US, psychic warfare and silent weapons are also banned, but this does not prevent their development.

Directed energy weapons are a type of *emerging* military technology that use focused energy, such as lasers, microwaves or particle beams, to attack targets. These weapons have reportedly been tested and developed for military applications, and some are already in use or in the process of development as budgets and some sources say.

R. Duncan and Mind Hacking Group state that the S.A.T.A.N. website interface is rare in everyday life. It doesn't require typing, moving a mouse or touching a screen. Some voice commands are used, but voice recognition is not traditional. The computer interface code listens to the inner vocal commands of the audiocortex using technology similar to that developed by the Sandford Research Institute (SRI) in the 1970s and NASA's research on the pre-cognitive motor pathways in the throat, and then categorizes these pre-cognitive vocal *intentions* into phonemes, words and sentences.

It is believed that the S.A.T.A.N. directed energy weapon could use various forms of electromagnetic radiation or high-frequency waves to produce devastating effects on electronic equipment, communications systems and even humans.

According to some sources, the weapon could also "cause extreme pain, intense suffering or mental and physical damage to specific targets without leaving visible traces", making its effects difficult to detect or prove.

In addition, there is speculation that it could be used for mental torture by inducing anxiety, constant pain or other effects on the psyche. Research on psychological manipulation and brainwashing torture has been the subject of intense debate and investigation within psychology and behavioral studies. Robert Duncan's *Project: Soul Catcher* explores the use of advanced technologies to control the mind by manipulating physical and emotional pain. The research shows that target individuals are often subjected to stimuli with the aim of collecting data to analyze human reactions to pain and fear. One of the many elements reported in the study is the use of a woman suffering from severe premenstrual syndrome as a subject for pain recording. In other words, the electromagnetic activity of the body was recorded at that moment and then played back to other individuals. Another hypothesis, that of pain transmission through neural empathization, is described below.

Recent scientific studies, such as those published by *Speroff et al.* 2019 in the *Journal of Clinical Endocrinology*, show that PMS (premenstrual syndrome) is a complex phenomenon with neurohormonal implications, affecting not only women's physical but also their emotional state.

The chronic pain and emotional distress experienced by the victims in the studies could thus be recognized as significant psychological *stimuli* that affect not only the individual, but can be transferred to others through mind control methods and advanced neurostimulation technology.

Pain without touch - is a form of torture that does not involve direct physical contact, but can be transferred through advanced technological devices.

Research has shown that modern technologies can induce psychic pain and discomfort by stimulating certain regions of the brain without physical contact. These techniques could involve the use of devices that manipulate the perception of pain, making the phenomenon described by Mr. Duncan possible.

Studies of empathy and the transmission of negative emotions in groups of individuals are also supported by research in affective neuroscience.

In the research of Decety and Jackson (2004)[9], it has been shown that people can feel and *transmit the* pain of others through a process called neural empathy, in which the activation of specific neural networks in one person can lead to the activation of the same networks in the brain of another person who witnesses that pain.

Decety and Jackson used functional magnetic resonance imaging (fMRI) to examine which areas of the brain are activated when a person observes someone experiencing pain.

In this context, participants were exposed to images of people in physical pain (e.g. being pricked or kicked) and observed their brain activity.

The results of the study showed that when participants observed pain in others, the same areas of the brain were activated as if they were experiencing pain themselves. These areas include, in particular, the **insula**[10] and the **anterior cingulate cortex**, which are involved in pain perception and processing. This phenomenon suggests that

---

[9] **Decety and Jackson,** *The Functional Architecture of Human Empathy* Article in Behavioral and Cognitive Neuroscience Reviews - June 2004 DOI: 10.1177/1534582304267187 - Source: PubMed
[10] *The insula is* a brain structure located deep inside the brain, involved in a variety of functions, including the perception of pain, emotions, taste and the processing of sensory information.

not only do we perceive others' pain from a cognitive perspective, but we also experience a form of emotional pain, which is the process of neural empathy.

Researchers concluded that neural empathy plays a crucial role in how people emotionally connect with and understand others' pain. This empathy is not just an emotional reaction, but also a neural reaction that reflects activity in the same brain regions that are activated when a person experiences pain directly.

This phenomenon may explain why one person's *mental pain* and negative emotions may be perceived by others in a group, even without direct contact or prior knowledge.

This research emphasizes the complex nature of pain manipulation and human mind control, addressing both the physical and emotional elements of torture and brainwashing. Although some authors, such as Duncan, suggest the existence of covert and unethical experiments, the majority of accepted scientific research to date does not support a complete theory of the technologies described.

Duncan also claims that the use of microwave torture can be used without trace and keeps the subject in pain for a long period without inducing death.

Chronic pain[11] is associated with multiple symptoms in about 1/3 of patients, including a combination of irritability, depression, anxiety, and sleep problems (Breivik et al., 2006; Yongjun et al., 2020; Mills et al., 2019).

But chronic pain is also associated with cognitive dysfunction, such as problems with attention, learning, memory and decision-making (Moriarty et al., 2011), as well as cardiovascular disease (Mills et al., 2019).

Chronic pain and its comorbidities lead to increased *disability* (Mutubuki et al., 2020), globally carrying the largest disability-related burden (Disease et al., 2018). The correlation between chronic pain and disability creates a huge cost to society of approximately **560-635 billion** dollars per year. These figures are double the annual costs of heart disease ($309 billion), cancer ($243 billion) and diabetes ($188 billion) (Gaskin and Richard, 2012), and back pain alone accounts for 1.7% of global national product per year (van Tulder et al., 1995).

These are impressive figures if we consider another important aspect: there are numerous patents for devices

[11] Neuroscience & Biobehavioral Reviews Volume 130, November 2021, Pages 125-146, *The anatomy of pain and suffering in the brain and its clinical implications*, Dirk De Ridder, Divya Adhia, Sven Vanneste https://www.sciencedirect.com/science/article/pii/S01497634210035 60

and systems to stimulate the central nervous system which, by stimulating a part of the brain, could induce pain sensations that do not have an organic cause of pain, nore is a result of an incident. Of course, the devices are only used for *beneficial* purposes, there is no doubt about that.

A mixture of overstimulation of the central nervous system, exposure to radiation, manipulation of the mind and emotions, microwaves, harmful bacteria, poor diet, viral infections, becomes hard on the body·

π

Year 1979-Tavistock Institute -Retrospective[12]

In 1979, "The young British intelligence recruits entering this building had no idea of the hell that awaited them," writes Richard Tomlinson in *Tomlison and the Russians*, a former MI6 spy who was part of the program.

"Little did they know that they would be forced into slavery to a demonic mind control program run by MI6 and authorized by Royal Freemasonry through the Tavistock Institute." R. Tomlinson, *Tomlinson and the Russians*

In 1979 at Powergen, twenty-one-year-old recruit Richard Tomlinson attended his first INSET training with British Intelligence; it was then that he was first shown a passport photograph of Vladimir Putin, which had been provided to him by one of his contacts, Oleg Gordievsky. Gordievsky, was the highest ranking K.G.B. officer to have betrayed and escaped to the West, being a Freemason in the Royal Lodge. *The training course* was led by Stella Remington, MI5, and John Scarlett, Controller General of MI6 modules. The two programs that were designed by the Tavistock Institute for graduate trainees of the British Secret Service were:

---

[12] Tavistock Institute: Social Engineering the Masses Paperback - September 22, 2015, by Daniel Estulin PhD

1. Programming "MI6 BEAST"

2. Programming "Smelly cheeses" in collaboration with Jonathan Livingstone Seagull.

The first refers to the *beast computer/cyborg* program inserted into each recruit's mind control program which was inserted during the recruitment training for both MI5 and MI6. One of the tasks set for the graduate trainees and the mind programmers running the course *devised* by *Royal Arch Freemasonry*, was *a treasure hunt*. The treasure hunt was to test their espionage skills and sadism. Part of the course was based on *an* ancient Roman *game* that soldiers played with prisoners.

It was a sadomasochistic *game* in which recruits were tortured and abused in a similar way to Roman prisoners the "method" being called the *Via Dolorosa*.

This program was devised by the Tavistock Institute and was designed with water as the main ingredient of torture. Programmers in the British secret service bring recruits into a near-death experience to make them submit. It's also a way of separating the weak from the strong. Programmers torture recruits repeatedly to break their Spirit.

The key to the program-an initiate is useless to them if they are unable to obey orders from above. Some people never recover from this experience. Symbolically, this is the process of birth, death and resurrection-the stages of the Cross. Most initiates/recruits are then taken to Jerusalem to walk the *Via Dolorosa* in order to reinforce this *programming-becoming Christ-like*." R. Tomlinson

Dr. Milgram[13] a professor at Yale, has done experiments on how people's morality can be converted when people in positions of power, authority are commanded to do unthinkable things. This can be seen in common situations where people excuse their actions by saying "I was just doing my job!".

Analyzing this technology one can observe several confusing aspects. The jargon and language used by satanic cults initiated by *certain government organizations*, come from the military and mythology, more specifically, black magic. This is done to mimic the occult sciences.

By substituting the common language for that of mythology, the agencies create a language barrier where the information is decoded, but also to those who write the scripts to be implanted, transmitted to humans via synthetic telepathy or *voice to skull*. Satanic cults were set up by

---

[13] *Obedience to Authority*: An Experimental View (Perennial Classics) - June 30, 2009, by Stanley Milgram

Michael Aquino to indoctrinate and manipulate the concept of *taking pride in doing evil, evil deeds for the government.*
R. Duncan, *Project: Soul Catcher*.

π

Programs and propaganda

For the understanding of these types of weapons and those presented before and further on, some precursor events and information should be mentioned, which could explain the technology that exists today and its connection with black magic.

Several international authors have emphasized that directed energy weapons imitate black magic, while other authors believe that all directed energy weapons have their origins in black magic.

Michael Hoffman, in *Secret Societies and Psychological Warfare*, writes: "Looking at the subject of mind control, one finds that the scope is broad and the methods sophisticated. Mind control has its origins in the institutional use of religion by some priests, secret societies, organizations not known to the public.

The mind control techniques that have been developed in our Western culture have been field-tested by various individuals belonging to different cults, institutions, organizations. The methods tested by the Inquisition were perfected by Dr. Josef Mengele during the Third Reich. Shortly thereafter, a mind control project called *Marionette*

Programming, imported from Nazi Germany, was revived as *Project Monarch.*

The core component of the Monarch program is the subtle manipulation of the mind, using extreme methods of trauma to induce a multiple personality disorder, known today as dissociative disorder. In the public testimony presented to the President's Committee on Radiation, there are startling allegations of severe torture and inhumane programs imposed on Americans and other citizens, especially children." *Secret Societies and Psychological Warfare*, **Michael Hoffman, Independent History and Research, 2001**

D. Estulin says in his book[14] , about this union of purely psychological and purely physiological aspects, which became the cornerstone of subsequent programs of intelligence agencies aimed at uncovering the secrets of the mind: the interface between the brain and the otherworld we call reality.

John Coleman, in his book *The Tavistock Institute for Human Relations: Shaping the Moral, Spiritual, Cultural, Political and Economic Decline of the United States* writes:

---

[14] Tavistock Institute: Social Engineering the Masses/Institutul *Tavistock: Ingineria Socială a Masselor* - September 22, 2015 byDaniel Estulin PhD,

"In addition to my own research in the field of *physical investigation*, Victor Marachetti, who worked for the CIA for 14 years, revealed the existence of a Tavistow-designed physical research program in which CIA agents attempted to contact the spirits of former agents who had died.

As I said in my monograph referred to above, I have had a wealth of personal experience in the *metaphysical* realms and I know for a fact that a large number of British and American intelligence agents are indoctrinated in this area. Tavistock calls it *behavioral science,* and it has advanced so rapidly in the last ten years that it has become one of the most important types of training that agents can take. In Tavistock's ESP/PES[15] (extrasensory perception) programs, each participant is *a volunteer* who agrees to have their personality *correlated* with extrasensory perception; in other words, they have agreed to help Tavistock find an answer to the question of why some people are psychic and others are gifted with ESP.

The aim of the exercise is to make every MI6 agent and

---

[15] ESP ESP extrasensory perception, also known as the sixth sense or cryptesthesia, is by definition *a supposed* paranormal ability related to the reception of information that is not obtained through the recognized physical senses, but perceived with the mind.

CIA highly psychic and highly developed extrasensory perception.

Because it's been many years since I've been directly involved in such matters, I consulted a colleague who is still *in the service* to find out how successful Tavistock had been with his experiments. He told me that Tavistock had perfected his techniques and that it was now possible to make select MI6 and CIA agents into perfect extra-sensory agents.

Here, it is necessary to explain that the CIA and MI6 maintain a very high degree of secrecy on such matters. Most of the intelligence agents in the programs are mostly members of the Illuminati and/or Freemasonry, or both. In short, the *long-range penetration* technique applied so successfully in the normal world is now being applied to the spirit world!

The Tavistock *Long Range Penetration* and *Inner Directional Conditioning* technique, developed by Dr. Kurt Lewin, whom I have already met several times, is primarily a program in which thought control is practiced on mass groups.

It was the British Army's Psychological Warfare Bureau, which handled propaganda in World War I, that set up the program. Large-scale propaganda was designed to convince

British workers that war was necessary. Another part was to convince the British public that Germany was an enemy and its leader a real demon.

This massive effort had to be launched between 1912 and 1914 because the British working class did not believe that Germany wanted the war. Just as the British people didn't want it, neither Germans did. All this public perception had to be changed."

As Peter Cuskie writes in *The Shaping of the Anglo-American SS by War*, "According to the post-war report on the assessment of OSS personnel, known as the *Assessment of Men*, John Rawling Rees and his Tavistock team at the *British War Office Selection Board*[16] were the ones who contacted

---

[16] *War Office Selection* Boards/War Office Selection *Boards*, or WOSBs (wosbees), were a scheme devised by British Army psychiatrists during World War II to select potential officers for the British Army. They replaced an earlier method, the Command Interview Board, and were the forerunners of today's army officer selection boards.

An experimental unit, the No. 1 War Office Selection Board (WOSB) was established in Edinburgh and opened on February 15, 1942. The first WOSB had its headquarters at the Institute of Genetics run by Francis Albert Eley Crewe, in the King's Buildings at the University of Edinburgh. Colonel J.V. Delahaye DSO was the first WOSB President.

Wilfred Bion was the board psychiatrist and **Eric Trist** the board psychologist. The first sergeants to be tested were Alex Mitchell and David O'Keefe, and the first military testing officer was Capt. W.N. Gray. Ten batches of candidates went through experimental testing. The new system required that, instead of a simple interview, the candidates should present themselves in a large provincial house to be tested for three days incorporating different methods.

In April 1942, the War Office expressed its satisfaction with the scheme and ordered that WOSBs be set up 'throughout Great Britain as soon as possible'. The bureaus were housed in provincial houses which had space to accommodate the

the OSS Office[17] in London to suggest that the special warfare organization adopt the selection and training methods proposed by the Tavistock Institute.

It was Rees who designed the OSS election brainwashing procedures, and Lewin who helped refine them. Rockefeller-sponsored Rees was the architect of a Rockefeller-sponsored insurgency-counter-insurgency project[18] promoted by the American financier.

The development of the CIA institution has essentially been geared toward a systematic infiltration of all existing mainstream institutions, an infiltration that is deliberate, a preparatory deployment aimed at establishing a quasi-

---

candidates and the tests applied to them. Subsequently, **WOSBs were set up abroad.** Boards were also established for the election of women officers for the Auxiliary Territorial Service, staffed by women, including women psychiatrists. Very little documentation of women's boards appears to have survived. **War Office Selection Boards (WOSB)**Date:1941-1987 Reference: SA/TIH/B/2/1/1/1 Part of: Tavistock Institute of Human Relations.

[17] The OSS-Office of Strategic Services was a United States intelligence agency during World War II. The OSS was formed as an agency of the Joint Chiefs of Staff to coordinate espionage activities behind enemy lines for all branches of the United States Armed Forces.

[18] An insurgency is an organized movement that aims to overthrow a legally constituted government through the use of subversion and armed conflict. The main target of insurgency is political power
Counterinsurgency. Military, paramilitary, political, economic, psychological or civic actions taken by the government to defeat the insurgency.
Counterinsurgency is by no means a foolproof technology or an exact science. They are both, in my humble opinion, methods that serve the same government-a self-serving government.

illegal fascist takeover with the help of prominent families involved in America's leadership.

Many of the future leaders of the CIA came from America's ruling families, from an endless group of bankers and industrialists such as DuPont, Vanderbilt, Bruce, Mellon, Archbold, Morgan and Roosevelt.

For example, Teddy Roosevelt's nephew, Quentin Roosevelt, was an OSS special operations officer in China, as was Winston Churchill's cousin, Raymond Guest. J.P.'s two sons. Morgan, Junius and Henry S. *were in charge of laundering all OSS funds and counterfeiting all OSS identity documents.*"

D. Estulin, Tavistock Institute and Human Relations.

π

It is strange how biblical prophecy, science, military technology and sociology seem to come together and converge at this important point in time in the development of our species.

"We tried to adapt evil as people perceive it, to create weaponry that attacks the information systems of the brain and body. We didn't know at the time what we were doing. I regret what I did."

Former DARPA employee and scientist.

"We are here to talk today about the fact that the brain is, and will be the battle field of the 21st century. End of story. You'll encounter a form of neurocognitive science that has been weaponized, not only in the military, but in professional, personal life. It is valid, valuable and already an operational plan. The brain is the current and future battle. What is new about this is how close this is. Increasingly, we see these things as weapons of mass destruction against a large mass of the population.

More specifically, they could be targeted perhaps, people at a level where they have direct attribution (blame), be employed undercover without attribution. Probably the one you've heard about most recently, most contemporary in the literature, is the possibility of using some form of directed energy to affect peripheral physiology and also to affect brain physiology and brain health, exactly what happened to personnel in the US Embassy in Havana and possibly in China. "

Dr. James Giordano DARPA Neurologist/Weapons Expert - presentation at the Modern Warfare Institute

π

2008- Nigeria

"You may go down and dine in the hotel, preferably with your fellow crewmates, but don't venture out on your own," the captain said seriously, like a protective father to the all female crew.

"I don't need to remind you that you are still in Nigeria," he reminded them, reinforcing the earlier idea. They all nodded in agreement, knowing what it was all about. They were escorted by special armed escorts, one military car each in front and behind the bus that transported them from the airport.

While waiting for the keys to the rooms that were to be returned to each member of the crew, the captain asked Iiris if she was all right.

She tried to reply, but could simply not speak, could not articulate a word. She cleared her voice a few times, apologized and replied hoarsely:

"I don't know what's wrong with me, but I feel like I have something in my throat. It's very strange. It's like there's something in my throat that prevents me from talking."

"Do you want me to give you an antibiotic? One pill is enough because it's very strong," the commander offered, knowing it would be better to avoid going to the clinics.

"I avoid taking antibiotics. Where is it from? What country did you buy it from?" asked Iiris skeptically.

"Germany. It's good. It gets the job done quickly," the commander replied convincingly.

"I think I'll take it because I don't think I've ever had these symptoms before. I have difficulty speaking, and when I try to do so I feel like something is slidding up and down and vice versa," she confessed probing the last few days to determine the causes of such a *sore* throat, but finding nothing conclusive.

For Iiris there were no coincidences. There had to be logical explanations and real causes. She was not weak. She was eating normally, nothing had changed in her diet, she had rested, she had not taken any other medication, she was mentally and emotionally well.

When she got to the room, she ate a piece of fruit and something very light to take the antibiotic.

In the evening the colleagues met on the ground floor of the hotel at the appointed time for dinner. After choosing their table and ordering their drinks, they headed for the beautifully laid out buffet. A veritable feast for kings and queens. After setting their plates they headed towards the table they were seated.

Meanwhile, at a neighboring table, some locals sat watching them intently. One stared at Iiris.

The women had started to discuss about what had happened on the flight and the local traditions. They were caught up in the conversation when a local approached from the next table, determined to address them.

"You! You come with me to my table!" he said to Iiris in a tone typical of Africans.

"Are you talking to me? Or all of us?" Iiris asked indignant at his impudence and to take the time to formulate a proper response and not send him back to his origins. She was still on duty time, even if she wasn't working.

"Yes, I'm talking to you. You get up from the table and come so I can introduce you to one of my boys," the African said, glaring at her.

She telepathically sent him a refrigerator full of all the *goodies* for a few seconds so as not to project a stool into his head in reality due to her growing irritability. She arched her eyebrows contemptuously and looking him straight in the eye replied in a tone to more throw the plate after him:

"First of all, you don't talk to me like that!!! If you ever open your mouth and insult me like that again, turn around and go back to your table, but not before apologizing for bothering me. You haven't introduced yourself, you come and act as if we are here for something other than dinner and you have the nerve to insult us. What is it with you people, *anyway*? You don't look like regulars, I see you haven't ordered anything, as if you've come here for another reason. Do I really need to call the police and the hotel security?", Iiris *spat* at him the words with a tone and visibly irritated after scanning the area and noticing that not even the staff in charge of the buffet was around. She continued.

"And in answer to your impertinent request. I'm not coming to your table, and I don't want to meet anyone, because I'm engaged."

"You say you're engaged. Where's your ring?" questioned the curious but phlegmatic man. Iiris had just very little to losing her temper. She couldn't believe she had to explain herself in front of a stranger and she was beginning to find his insistence strange.

She didn't take her engagement ring when traveling to avoid unpleasant events. She traveled everywhere, and some destinations were dangerous. So, she left the ring at the base where she lived.

"I don't have to prove to you that I'm engaged. You have to take my word for it. I don't have the ring on me. It's upstairs in the room," she replied irritably.

"Listen! I'm the manager of the boy next table. I've trained him, he's strong and good and Man**aster United bought him. My boy's really all right. He plays for Man**aster United, don't you understand? He's got his eye on you!" said the man angry at being turned down and irritated at not being humored.

"Congratulations to him for his performance, but as I said I am engaged", said Iiris trying to get out of the situation and looking for a way out.

Her colleagues watched the scene without saying anything. She looked at them hoping that one of them would say something.

"But I'm curious about one thing. How did you come to me so determined? You haven't ordered anything from the restaurant, you've been looking insistent ever since you came as if you'd come specifically for something. And then this insistence. Why are you so determined to convince me? It seems illogical and it's disrespectful, and on closer inspection your man doesn't have the air of some incurable romantic, I would even say he doesn't seem interested in me the very little. Can you tell me what this is really about?

And then let's say I believe your intentions...Even if I wasn't engaged, I wouldn't have come to the table. In my culture that is not practiced, and for us it is very rude for a man to expect a woman to come to a table full of men and all strangers. It is unacceptable to me!

There is a solution though, but I'm not promising to take any action. Tell *your boy* to write down his phone number, and maybe sometime, MAYBE, who knows how and when I'll text him. And that's it! No promises!", Iiris replied, seeing with her mind's eye how that note would end up in his colleague's pocket.

A beautiful South African half-breed, but also hoping to end the conversation and get out of the strange situation.

The manager had returned with a torn note from a math page with *his boy's* number written on it and *Live in London written* under the number.

The priestess did not understand his insistence. It wasn't natural and *his boy* didn't even show a hint that he liked her. Something was wrong.

Her colleagues looked at her with mixed emotions. To end the episode, she said to them in a reproachful tone: "We wouldn't have got rid of him and insisted. Security isn't here, not even the serving staff. I will never call him! And why didn't you intervene in some way? It concerns us all after all!".

Her fellow Indian colleagues lowered their eyes as if to apologize, but Iiris saw something in their eyes, something strange, a flicker of something manifesting through them.

She gave the note to Tasha, hoping she had done something good. She said a short prayer for Tash, hoping it would be a good omen.

Much later she would learn about that sinister *modus operandi*, and that she was being monitored from an early age. She was to learn how certain women were used for the interests of certain organizations, and how they were *accidentally* placed in various circles without them having the slightest suspicion. Coincidences, coincidences, but after the second coincidence investigation, investigation...

That same evening Iiris returned to her room, tired after the flight and the events. She had the same strange sensation in her throat as if she had an obstruction. She wasn't breathing very well.

She laid on the side to breathe better. About half past two in the morning, he suddenly woke up, barely breathing and coughing like a fire.

She looked at the clock and wanted to call a doctor at the front desk. He knew it would take at least 30 minutes to get to the hotel, and without air he could only last 2-3 minutes. She thought about going down to the front desk to get her CPR or something, to use the defibrillator in case she was no longer conscious.

By her calculations not much would have been solved. She calmed down immediately, remembering she had a nose. She began to breathe through nose. She calmed down. She wasn't panicky, but she had woken up so suddenly and in such unexpected circumstances that she hadn't had time to think much.

She went into the bathroom, bent down and coughed as hard as she could to force the obstruction. He patted between her shoulder blades for as long as she could and then positioned herself over the toilet. The obstruction started to move, but stopped somewhere in the area of the oropharynx. Panic was setting in, but Iiris was trained to find solutions in any circumstance but now she didn't know what it was.

"Really God? In here? Away from family and friends? She was already running the movie. Couldn't it be somewhere else?" she spoke to God, though she felt a reassurance inside that it wasn't time.

"What am I supposed to do at this hour?"

She was urged to cough again, more forcefully. She did so, and just as the obstruction was about to come out, it stopped so that she could no longer breathe through her mouth or nose. Exasperated, and calculating how long she was without air, she coughed once more with all her might. Out came something gray, something that looked like thread, something that wasn't food. A lump of something that couldn't be categorized in any way. What was certain was that the thing looked like something that wasn't organic.

"Seriously?! What is this mess?????"

"Voodoo," she heard a voice, and sensed someone looking through her eyes. Iiris knew that the thought didn't belong to her because she didn't believe in such a thing, an association like that wasn't specific to her, and the voice was male.

Thanks for your help, God! But what happened?

Whose voice was that? And how did he know he was in that situation? How did he "see"?

She had received a suggestive calming urge, and the perception that she would find out later. She could perceive soul interference and telepathic interference. At the time she was unaware of the control that certain factions and other organizations, and others, exerted over innocent people, people gifted with certain abilities, people they were using without their awareness.

She was peaceful, she was with God. She felt him. God would never speak to her. He would communicate subtly, silently and warmly.

She later understood much more.

Most "abnormal events" had an explanation, an answer, except one.

Only one event could not be explained. An event that occurred in 1996 when she sensed a life other than the perceived human one, a bios but of something or someone communicating excellent telepathically. She wanted to see for herself, but that something, someone had jumped from the balcony of her house. She heard it as it stepped on the balcony planks and then on the boards of the basement porch and then as it *landed* on the cement. It was between 2-3 in the morning. The dog didn't smell it, either.

Iiris laid on the bed and tried to fall asleep. She couldn't, she felt restless and pulled out a magazine to read a few lines hoping sleep would take her. She opened the magazine to an article about zombies. As soon as she started reading, she closed the magazine and thought to herself:

My God, don't I have anything else to read? Who believes in stories like that anymore?

As she laid on her bed, she heard footsteps coming from the balcony door towards her window. She was sure it was her brother. She waited for him to approach the window and say something to her. Footsteps stopped in front of the window. It had a mosquito net. Iiris was on summer vacation and had just come from the disco.

"Paul!" *Why does he keep joking like that? Why doesn't he say anything?*

" Paul? Paul?" she asked, waiting for her brother to answer. Iiris looked from the bed to the window and felt the bios. A chill that seemed to be a sensation of fear came over her. She was surprised because she had no reason to be.

"Paul, why don't you answer? What's gotten into you?"

Paul is on duty, Iiris heard the thought she was about to register as her own.

Wait, I didn't know Paul was on duty. How would I know that? That's when she felt the pressure she was already used to and the feeling of fear, making it hard to move.

Whatever it is, I'm not staying in bed. I'm going to see for myself if something's there. There must be. I heard footsteps and had that strange feeling. There must be an explanation.

In a few seconds he was out of bed, and walking towards the reception room where the entrance to the balcony was, he perceived himself emerging from an invisible bubble and heard a thought: *Wake your mother!*

Iiris, without realizing it, went to her mother's room to wake her up, inadvertently giving that someone, something time to run away.

She heard him step on the planks, onto the blackboard and jump. Earlier, when she was looking out the window trying to catch a glimpse of her *brother's* silhouette, hoping it was a bad joke, she perceived it as someone, something nearly six feet tall, maybe more.

She still to this day could not explain what it could be. A someone, something that was influencing through fear because she felt him wanting to induce fear in her, to not move from the bed and come to the balcony. Someone who was reading her thoughts in real time and inserting thoughts in real time. Loud and clear. She cried of nervousness and helplessness. It was too much. Too much had accumulated. She didn't understand what was happening to her and why.

Later she would learn that a certain faction had a fierce interest in the plasma activity in the area of certain people. She would hear about that faction that same year. That same faction had literally always hunted those who, like herself, had had the vision that Iiris had on Good Friday. She would find out 20-some years later that that vision was important to an order that apparently didn't get along too well with that faction. The oldest Christian order in existence, a sovereign order. She also understood the atrocious struggle against Christianity practiced in truth, virtue and love. According to the details of that vision that wretched faction (God forgive me!) knew something about Iiris they exploited to their own advantage many years to come. The age at which the vision usually would take place would be around 15-16, and it was only *shown* to certain female representatives. (see EMPs and their effects on UFOs)

CIA and satanic cults

The mythology of the end of the 20th century is extremely coherent, even if the forms it takes vary from case to case, victim to victim. Of course, the CIA exists and their mind control programs, from Bluebird to Artichoke to Artichoke to MKULTRA, are already public knowledge.

Their history of political assassinations and overthrowing foreign governments is also well documented and archived. Satanic cults, or perhaps more correctly occult secret societies, also exist and are a matter of public interest; their attempts to contact higher entities through mystical rituals are also well known and documented.

All this, together with espionage activities, forms *a* dense *salad* of paranoia, prestige, and power that combines secret government work with the occult rituals and manipulation of dark forces that we have been analyzing. The secret handshake and the code of intelligence agencies are symbols of a power not accessible to ordinary people.

"Intelligence officers and cultists have a lot in common. Secrecy is a way of life for both spy and magician:

-both use codes and codenames; both claim to have access to mysteries not available to the general public

-both claim they can influence events remotely with their special abilities and powers; both specialize in manipulating reality

-both are aware that things are not always what they appear to be and both are ruthless, amoral and immoral in the pursuit of their goals.

And one could so easily manipulate the perception of reality that one eventually comes to the realization that Truth itself is a malleable thing. This is the illusion.

"So, it was only natural that the cultist and the spy would gravitate towards each other and try to learn from each other." **Peter Levenda, Sinister Forces**

This control of reality, of the perception of reality and the creation of *consensual reality* is a powerful political tool and has been since antiquity, when proverbial sorcerers could create solar eclipses simply by knowing when one was going to occur and acting accordingly. To control and manipulate the reality of the masses, what is called psychological warfare is used. From controlling a person's perception of reality to getting them to act on it is only one step.

The Germans were among the first to study psychological warfare; it became after the war inextricably intertwined with propaganda and communications, and eventually, it blended into acts of terrorism: assassinations, acts of sabotage, torture and interrogations in the Tavistock Institute's domain.

As psychological warfare has become more sophisticated and intelligence services both more creative and more demanding, new techniques have been developed and practically codified. All these techniques share a common ontological goal: the manipulation of perceptions and the co-creation of reality. Once Pandora's box was opened, it was no longer possible to close it. The temptation was too great.

For those who wanted to play God, here's the important thing: they could play with the elements of creation in such a way that magical transformations could take place. As the men in the OSS, CIA and military intelligence, overseen by Tavistock, transformed themselves from armchair scientists (as most of them were before the war years) into soldiers fighting on all fronts of the Cold War, becoming in a very real sense, magicians, "the CIA's mind control projects themselves represented an assault on consciousness and reality not seen in history since the age of the philosopher kings and their court alchemists.'' **P.Levenda** *Sinister Forces/Forțe sinistre*

The CIA and Tavistock were opening a Pandora's box of demonic forces: the black box of consciousness.

Techniques included drugs, various forms of hypnosis and even more extreme measures, such as those developed by Montreal's Dr. Ewen Cameron, procedures known as ''psychic driving,'' which involve drastic sensory deprivation in an attempt to erase consciousness and record over, *tape a* used *cassette*. It's the story of a modern Frankenstein, or a laboratory full of Frankensteins, and the monsters they make: monsters that roam the streets of our cities today.

To quote Peter Levenda: ''The complexity of human experience is such that one can only wonder what trigger mechanisms exist in the environment - on television, in newspapers and magazines, and even on the internet - that suggest to these victims, ways of behaving that are dangerous to themselves and to us.

It would only be a matter of time before mind control researchers would begin delving into the records of occultists, magicians, witches, voodoo priests and shamans to isolate techniques that have been used since forgotten times to supplant a person's normal, comfortable, everyday consciousness. All for the purpose of replacing a man's old personality with a powerful, all-knowing, sometimes violent and always deceptive personality, and to use these alterations to uncover deep memory actions, for MK ULTRA was, at its core, a memory attack aimed at **creating new, false memories and eradicating old, dangerous ones.**

In the pursuit of perfection and for intelligence purposes, what was required of the MK ULTRA program was to obtain a method to manipulate memory. But in exploring the mind and developing techniques to unlock secrets, the agency unwittingly stepped into territory that had been the domain of religion, of mysticism for thousands of years.

After the CIA incorporated drugs into the program and bizarre techniques of sensory deprivation, all the conditions were met of a serious occult experience found in cults as disparate as Eleusis in Greece, Tantra in India, Shamanism, Taoism in China, Jewish Kabbalah, even the relatively modern phenomenon of European ceremonial magic - as OTO, and individuals such as Aliester Crowley. As mythologists such as Carl Jung, Mircea Eliade and others have demonstrated, there is a great similarity 'in technology' between these obscure practices, and this similarity exists for a reason." **D. Estulin,** *Tavistock Institute: Social Engineering of the Masses*

The obscure doctrine and methods of an abandoned science lie at the heart of this study, as it reveals the mechanisms by which society in general and individuals in particular have been manipulated by forces beyond their comprehension.

"Thus, the magician is both interrogator and interrogatee. He is charged with manipulating and controlling the environment, but not for the effect it will have on anyone else, but only on himself.

What the CIA has done in its interrogation manual - itself the product of MK ULTRA - is to separate the magician from the ultimate goal of occultism (spiritual perfection and elevated consciousness) by directing him to focus all the powers of occult techniques on the magician:

- a subject whose will is not to be manipulated but is informed that this is happening, in order to manipulate both him and his environment

- to change the subject to something more useful to the interrogators

- to make him a mortal danger to the subject's own people.

It is in the jargon of the occult, of black magic. And black magic is in the service of the state". **Peter Levenda,** *Sinister Forces.*

The doors of perception were opened not only by drugs such as mescaline, LSD and psilocybin, but also by séances, shamans and secret rituals.

All had become tools for the CIA elements, and their attacks on memory and consciousness opened the doors of perception and, letting the light in, let the darkness out. Drugs, shamanism and the occult. The dark realm of John Rawlings Rees, Nazi doctors, Hollywood and the music industry, the CIA, MI6, the Israeli services, initiation sessions. With psychedelics, they have disturbed the slumber of ancient forces, and the world will never be the same again.

Coming back.

Below you will find a short list with explanations for some of the words used by satanic cults and their equivalence in secret agencies. (*Project: Soul Catcher* p227). As written by R. Duncan, these names are used when the weapon called S.A.T.A.N. is used.

1) To cast a **spell** or say a curse-is to run the S.A.T.A.N. program on them. This results in a false-weapon-induced

state that feels real, like *dark clouds of doom* being correlated with altered behavior that is detrimental to human survival.

2)To possess by means of a **demon**- rumination-values and negative vocabulary through A.L.I.C.E. programs and real time mentally induced T.A.M.I.'s or psychic/psi (paranormal) warriors. Demons that distract and destroy.

3) **Medusa** turned humans to stone.

Hypnosis and army zombies are *projects* that have been worked on to keep people trapped in their own physical and mental suffering so that they are unable to do or think for themselves.

In this case, people perceive a feeling of extreme fear or the perception of a mental war on which the idea that it cannot be won is also induced. They are held captive in a social delusion, desperately trying to keep them in the salad of social networks, fake news, induction of helplessness, restriction of freedom by diminishing discernment, preformation of an opinion on a subject, replacement of the thinking process by induction of thoughts.

4) **The sirens**, lure their listeners with *their enticing songs* (the frequencies that induce illusory states). The desire to know the truth is the lure they sometimes use to misdirect people and induce a greater sense of frustration.

Scams like "Take your pill. We're here to help you.", are scenarios that secret services use.

5)**Psychological vampires** drain the life force from a person. This is *accomplished* through the loss of hope, long lasting psychic torture and the shattering of the human spirit. It is the "ultimate" goal of brainwashing and advanced interrogation techniques.

As Levenda writes in Sinister Forces, "There must have been a level at which U.S. government leaders identified with or at least admired the Nazis. There must have been a point at which the crimes of the Holocaust were seen as a minor distraction and a public relations issue that was overshadowed by the allure of the perfectly managed superstate of the Third Reich. There must have been an understanding that the ideologies of America and Nazi Germany were more similar than the ideologies of America and the Soviet Union. There is no other way of interpreting what happened at the end of the war: morally, what happened can only be considered a war crime in itself.

"Washington decision-makers knew that the next major conflict would be between the United States and the Soviet Union. It was vitally important that top German scientists working on the super-secret V-1 and V-2 projects and nuclear weapons technology be brought to American shores, out of Russian range and, perhaps most importantly, integrated into the service of the United States.

"By that time several wartime intelligence operations had been set in motion. The best known was Operation Paperclip. Most people who know about the Nazi Operation *Paperclip* know that it was a program to bring in Nazi scientists to help the United States with its space program. However, Paperclip, and the subsequent recruitment of Nazis, was much more than rocket science. It also recruited Nazi medical personnel, as well as experts in psychological warfare and, along with Gehlen Organization spies, assassins and saboteurs.

The *Paperclip* story is long and very complex; it involves *the alphabet soup of* intelligence agencies and programs, from CROWCASS (Central Registry of War Crimes and Security Suspects) to CIC, SIS, OSS, CIA, JIOA and many others. These include dozens of countries, their intelligence agencies, armies, political parties, the Roman Catholic Church and criminal justice systems. By the end of the war, an entire Waffen SS division from the Ukraine, as well as thousands of Nazi scientists, many of them accused of war crimes, who participated in some of the worst atrocities of the war, had managed to settle in the United States, South America and the Middle East." *Sinister Forces/Forțe Sinistre*, **The nine, Book 1, Peter Levenda, Trineday Press, p.134-135, May 2011**

There was another dimension to the German scholar that was not discussed so much publicly and went strangely unnoticed, but it was recorded in the Captured German Documents section of the National Archives, but the first evidence of it appeared in the memoirs of Himmler's astrologer - Wilhelm Wulff.

He speaks of the Nazi intentions to reproduce the mental state of the Japanese soldier, eager and willing to risk his life for his country. Added to this intention is *the reproduction of* the Chinese communist soldier who throws himself like a wave unthinkingly into any situation for his country.

So, Paperclip Project scientists have been involved in military and CIA mind control programs, such as Friedrich

Hoffman, a Nazi chemist who advised the CIA on matters related to psychotropic substances used in brainwashing".
Sinister Forces, **The Nine, Book 1, Peter Levenda, Trineday Press, p.134-135, May 2011**

π

E-man and neural dust

"We can hack not just computers. We can hack human beings and other organisms. Organisms, whether viruses or bananas or humans, are really just biochemical algorithms. And we learn how to decipher these algorithms. When the infotech revolution meets the biotech revolution, what you get is the ability to hack human beings. So, what do you need to hack a human being? You need two things. You need a lot of computing power. And you need a lot of data, especially biometric data, not data about what I buy or where I go, but data about what's going on inside my body and inside my brain.

And perhaps the most important invention for the fusion of infotech and biotech is the biometric sensor that translates biochemical processes in the body and brain into electronic signals that a computer can store and analyze."

Yaval Noah Harari Historian and technology philosopher/World Economic Forum Presentation: *Will the future be human?*

"One of the newest developments is that nanoparticulate matter can be stabilized for distribution. Now, we're aware of what nanoparticulate matter is. It's that matter which exists on a scale of one times ten to the minus ninth. Very,

very small. Smaller than a cell. And we can manufacture materials that have discrete properties that can be controlled by virtue of bioengineering and their physical chemistry.

To auto aggregate, to be able to aggregate in particular areas based upon their biological and their chemical sensitivity. But now we go one step further. Most recently, just a few weeks ago, it was announced that you could then aerosolize nanomaterials. And go one step further, I can create small robotic units controllable robotic units at the nanoscale and that these two can be aerosolized to create a nano swarm of biopenetrable materials that you cannot see, that can penetrate all but the most robust biochemical filters, that are able to integrate themselves through a variety of membranes, mucus membranes in wherever, mouth, nose, ears, eyes, can be then uptaken into the vascular system to create clumping.

Can affect the vascular system of the brain or can directly diffuse into the brain space, and these can be weaponized."

Dr. James Giordano DARPA Neurologist/Weapons Expert-Presentation at the Modern War Institute

DARPA's Electrical Prescriptions (ElectRx) program is focused, among other things, on overcoming current limitations and developing interface technologies suitable for biosensing and neuromodulation of peripheral nerves.

A group of researchers funded by DARPA[19] and led by the Department of Electrical Engineering and Computer Science at the University of California, Berkeley, has achieved a significant innovation: a millimeter-sized wireless device, small enough to be implanted in individual nerves, capable of sensing the electrical activity of nerves and muscles in the body and using ultrasound for power and communication. The developed devices, called *neural powder*, were first tested *in vivo* on rodents.

Neural dust represents a radically different approach than the traditional use of radio waves for wireless communication with implanted devices, explains Doug Weber, manager of the ElectRx program[20].

Because the soft tissues of the human body are mostly salt water, **sound waves** can pass through these tissues and can

---

[19] The Defense Advanced Research Projects Agency is a research and development agency of the United States Department of Defense responsible for developing emerging technologies for military use

[20] DARPA, official website, *Implantable "Neural Dust" Enables Precise Wireless Recording of Nerve Activity*
https://www.darpa.mil/news/2016/implantable-neural-dust

be precisely focused to deep nerve targets, unlike radio waves.

By using ultrasound to communicate with the neural dust, the sensors can be smaller and placed deeper in the body, by needle injection or other non-surgical methods.

The neural dust particle prototypes measure 0.8 millimeters x 3 millimeters x 1 millimeter, and the researchers estimate that by using customized parts, they could make particles 1 cubic millimeter or even smaller, up to 100 microns per side.

The small size allows multiple sensors to be placed close together for more precise recording of nerve activity at various locations of a nerve or nerve group. The piezoelectric crystal is essential for neural dust projection.

Each sensor contains just three main parts: a pair of electrodes for measuring nerve signals, a customized transistor for signal amplification, and a piezoelectric crystal that converts the mechanical energy of external ultrasound waves into electrical energy and communicates the recorded nerve activity. The neural powder system also includes an external transcription plate that utilizes ultrasound for powering and communicating with the particles, emitting pulses of ultrasonic energy and capturing the reflected pulses.

"One of the most attractive features of neural dust sensors is that they are completely passive. Because there are no batteries to change, there is no need for additional surgery after the initial implant," Weber said.

This prototype was developed in the first phase of the ElectRx program, and the research team will continue to work on miniaturizing the sensors, ensuring biocompatibility, increasing the portability of the transcription board, and improving signal processing when multiple sensors are placed close together.

Source DARPA website, article: *Implantable "Neural Dust" Enables Precise Wireless Wireless Recording of Nerve Activity/Implantable Neural Dust enables wireless recording of nerve activity*, 03.08.2016

Some sources claim that if the technology described under the DARPA ElectRx program were used to remotely control target individuals, it could involve such possibilities as manipulating a person's nerve activity or physiological functions through implantable devices. In this case, the neural powder could be used to influence or modulate electrical signals in nerves or muscles, or possibly the brain, which could affect a person's behavior, movements, or even mental states.

By using ultrasound for power and communication, this technology could be controlled remotely without the need for complicated implants or repetitive invasive procedures, as no batteries would be needed and no further surgery would be required. This would mean that a small, passive device could be used to monitor and, in theory, manipulate nerve activity without the person being aware of the process.

Below is proposed "a method of *writing and saving* the human soul by means of electronic chips, the inventor claiming that electronic immortality can be achieved.

From here up to the extraction, capturing of the soul, breath and the connection of the electromagnetic activity of the body (IoT-internet of things) to a synthetic intelligence, it was just a step. In our opinion *the theories* presented in this patent and beyond, were an indirect warning of the control that certain factions have over humans, strategically and subtly placing the blame on others.

Personally, we take in consideration the theory that this control has been practiced for millennia, and somehow the theory of holding souls captive in this space would make sense in this context. They believe in the law of cause and effect, which causes them to publicize what they are about to do or do, thus believing that they are absolved of the effect. This is obviously just a theory. This does not apply to natural law.

Innocent people are often used blindly, unbeknownst to them, by the *participants in the subsystem,* urging them to actions that serve their ends, and innocent people end up calling that accumulation of actions fate and paying the price as innocents.

What's described below is part of the technology that's already within reach, sources say.

This said to process data and record it in an international bank where everyone has their personal file and a *digital* twin/digital *twin.* It remains at the theory stage as no official has confirmed, but this does not mean that we cannot question and ask the right questions and demand declassification of such secrets if they are secret and if they are being used without our knowledge and consent. After all, we have the right to know the truth.

Note: The patent you will read about below is listed as having an abandoned status, but what is described appears to be something already in practice. The intention is not to misinform, but on the contrary to shed light where some people need it, to offer possible explanations for seemingly inexplicable experiences. Some of us have been guinea pigs without our consent, and under the pretext of such things as initiations, evolutionary healing processes, karma or *other nonsense* induced to make these experiences more tolerable, we have nonconsensually accepted *the cloud of misfortune* that has followed us without reason. It is time for justice.

If you read carefully, you will notice that most of the proposals are already present in most of the devices we have at hand. It should be a wake-up call, not a normalization of this. Nobody has the right to our autonomy.

United States of America, Patent application

Pub. Nr.: US 200900626267777A1[21]

Application Date: Dec 20, 2006Pub. Date: Mar. 5, 2009

21

https://patentimages.storage.googleapis.com/c3/1e/e1/b6d3fe239258a2/US20090062677A1.pdf

Status: *abandoned(?)*

Method of recording and saving the human soul for human immortality and installation for it

Inventor shows that a human soul is just the information present in the human brain. He offers a method of rewriting the human brain on electronic chips. This method allows the modeling of a human soul to achieve human immortality. This method does not damage the brain, but works to expand and *improve* it.

This method of *writing and saving* the human soul includes:

- writing the impressions that the person sees during their lifetime using a micro video recorder on a portable memory stick;

- writing the sounds the person speaks and hears through the microphone (?);

- writing the person's physical conditions using micro-sensors;

-time and date;

- writing the person's body position and so on.

An installation using the method comprises the following devices: video camera on the human head, microphone, computer (chip) for data processing, portable memory in a person's body and connected to the portable memory;

portable recorder for writing the movie of life located in the human body and connected to the computer and the portable memory; micro-sensors for writing the physical and environmental conditions of the person; a clock for time recording, micro-sensors for positions of the human body; navigation system, long-life memory with large storage capacity and so on.

This method allows the molding of a human soul to achieve immortality. This method does not damage the brain, but works to expand and *improve it.*

Immortality is *every person's fondest dream and greatest desire*(?).

And no matter what heavenly existence in the afterlife is promised by religion, the vast majority of people want to stay and enjoy life here on Earth as long as possible. The inventor shows that a real immortality can only be electronic (?). In his previous works, the author showed that the problem with immortality can only be solved by changing biological man into an artificial form.

Such an immortal person made of chips and supersolid materials **E-man**, as it has been called in the author's articles, will have incredible advantages over conventional humans.

An E-man will not need food, shelter, air, sleep.

Its brain will be powered by radio isotope batteries (which will run for decades) and muscles that will be powered by tiny nuclear engines. Such a being will be able to travel in space and walk on the sea floor without *aqualungs*.

It will change its face and figure. He will have superhuman strength and will easily communicate over long distances to acquire huge amounts of knowledge in seconds (by rewriting his brain). His mental abilities and capacities will increase by millions of times. It will be possible for such a person to travel huge distances at the speed of light.

Such a person's information could be transported to other planets with a laser beam and then placed in a new body *(information is already being transmitted with laser technology)*.

The main problem of immortality

Rewriting information from the brain (soul) onto electronic chips: it is impossible to do this with current technology (2009).[22]

---

[22] Above you read about DARPA projects and neural programs, nanoparticles and their applications, their aerosolization.

Shaping the soul for a concrete person

As has been said, directly rewriting a human mind (the human soul) on chips is very complex.

In order to solve the main problem of immortality, the author offers a method of *molding the soul of* a created person. This method requires no intervention in the brain of a particular person. This method can be applied immediately in the present.

The industry produces cheap, penny-sized micro video recorders, grain-sized micro telephones, and micro sensors for vital signs (breathing, palpitations, blood pressure, skin resistance, sweating, movement of body parts, etc.). These measurements make it easy to record not only his physical state, but also his moral state (joy, pleasure, sorrow, grief, anxiety, nervousness, etc.).

We can now measure and record brain commands and produce small cards with four gigabytes of memory.

It would be easy to attach a video recorder and microphone to a man's forehead and then attach body sensors and record everything he sees, hears, speaks, his feelings, reactions and activity. [23]

---

[23] J. Giordano, DARPA, talked about the nano swarm that can penetrate any material.

And then rewrite this information on your personal hard disk (long-term memory of large storage capacity) at the end of each day. As a result, there is a record of the most important part of our soul-life history, feelings, environment, behaviors and actions. This would be more detailed than what is captured by the real human because humans forget many facts, feelings, emotions and personal interactions. Electronic memory would not forget anything from the past. It would not forget any person or what they did.

For a while, biological and electronic humans will exist together. However, the distance between their capabilities will increase very rapidly. Electronic people will reproduce (multiply) themselves through the process of copying data *(you may wonder why there is a need for consent to use personal data?)*, they will learn instantly and will not need food or housing.

They will work for days in a row, in any conditions such as in space or at the bottom of the ocean. They will acquire new knowledge in a short time. They will pass this knowledge on to others who don't have enough time. The distance between biological and artificial intellect will reach a wide margin, so that biological people will understand nothing about new discoveries in science just as monkeys do not understand multiplication now even after many explanations.

The authors disagree with such an expression, but it is translated as it appeared in the patent.

Obviously, intelligent people will see that there will be a huge difference between the mental abilities of biological entities and electronic entities. They will try to transfer themselves into electronic form and the ratio between the biological and the electronic entity will rapidly change in favor of the electronic one.

A small number of exceptions will continue to live in their special enclaves designed for biological bodies. They will have no industrial strength or higher education and will begin to degrade.

Sound familiar? Keep in mind that the year of publication is 2009.

Naysayers can pass anti-transfer laws into an electronic human (as cloning is now banned in some states). However, who would give up immortality for themselves, especially while young and healthy? One could denounce immortality as blasphemy... The ability to live forever, to acquire life-enhancing knowledge, will also enable one to become a sovereign force in the Universe." Not!

Excerpt from the application

Pub. Nr.: US 2009006262677A1 [24]

This experiment, once long ago, was done. Negative interference leads to disasters that would destroy the world irreversibly if not intervened in time. That is why immortality is a *rare* gift, given to those of exceptional merit who have succeeded at the level of the human soul to transcend the trials of correcting those imperfections that could not provide a perfect balance. This is a veiled statement

After our experiences, we believe that the above experiment/patent has not been abandoned, but rather integrated into a larger project. E-brain. Also known as the Global Brain Project.

"What we're here to talk about today is the fact that the brain is and will be the 21st century battlescape. End of story. You will encounter some form of neurocognitive science that has been weaponized, not only in your military

---

24

https://patentimages.storage.googleapis.com/c3/1e/e1/b6d3fe239258 a2/US20090062677A1.pdf career, but in your personal professional lives. It is valid, valuable, and already an operational plan. The brain is the current and future battle. What's new about this is the in close nature of this.

Increasingly, we're not seeing these things as weapons of mass destruction against gross aspects of the population. More specifically, perhaps, might be targeting individuals on a level that allows either direct attribution or covert engagement with non attribution. Probably the one that you've heard about most recently, most contemporaneously in the literature, is the possibility to use some form of directed energy to affect physiology peripherally and also to affect the physiology and health of the brain. Case in point here, U. S. Embassy personnel in Havana and possibly in China."

Dr. James Giordano DARPA Neurologist/Weapons Expert - presentation at the Modern Warfare Institute

"How would people react if a Pentagon official told the truth and described these human experimentation and behavioral torture and assassination projects on the news? But because of the endless string of abuses, people are finally speaking out.

The psychology community has been used to get rid of some of the greatest thinkers of our time... It's been proven that the mind can be controlled under constrained conditions. Creating the illusion of free will and choice helps to calm the populace in any society, be it a fake democracy or a communist country. After all, we are only human animals, according to DARPA." **Robert Duncan,** *Project: The Soul Catcher*

On the OHCHR website[25] the document referring to electromagnetic harassment and torture presents the symptoms that **targeted individuals** most often report and experience. Predictably, the first reference is to American diplomats (Havana Syndrome), but it should be known that people all over the world are suffering and have been showing these symptoms for a long time without knowing the source of their suffering.

Notice that these people are called individuals, not persons (masks, fictitious). This difference is important. The term

[25] 1 Electromagnetic harassment with torturous patterns (electromagnetic torture, cybernetic torture or cybertorture): "the crime that people complain most about on the internet/social media"
https://www.ohchr.org/sites/default/files/Documents/Issues/Torture/Call/Individuals/ElectromagneticTorture.pdf

individual-that which cannot be divided, is something singular, something particular with all its characteristics, which are determinative of its individuality. It is a singular being or entity in a spatial and temporal sense. That is, whose individuality, soul cannot be "broken" (see MK Ultra program).

Among these symptoms you will find a resemblance to the projects previously mentioned by *experts in* the field of mental and implicit behavioral control.

Victims of electromagnetic stalking, often called Targeted Individuals or TI/Targeted *Individuals* report:

U.S. victims of electromagnetic harassment have provided comment to the Presidential Commission for the Study of Bioethical Issues (created by President Obama) in March and May 2011[26]. In Europe, the Ministry of Defense of Poland conducted a geographical analysis of complaints of Polish victims for electromagnetic attacks in 2016. Following correspondence with the Ministry, Polish victims have been heard by the Inspectorate of Innovative Defense Technologies of the Ministry of Defense. Among different protests against electromagnetic harassment/torture, two

---

26

https://www.ohchr.org/sites/default/files/Documents/Issues/Torture/Call/Individuals/ElectromagneticTorture.pdf international rallies have been held on the 29th August in 2019 and 2018. Victims of electromagnetic harassment, often called "Targeted Individuals" or "TIs" report:

1. Torturous routines such as head and body electromagnetic stimulation e.g. intense sudden contractions of (surface) muscle fibers equivalent to painful stimulus of being hit, different stimulation patterns generating miscellaneous effects e.g. pain, tingling, pins-and-needle effect and also intense heating, burning or itching sensations.

2. Artificial tinnitus, hearing voices and mental manipulation i.e. mental content presentation/insertion and extraction (personal thought content being repeated to them in an interval of a few seconds). 3. Manipulation via brain-to-brain interface: A remote human operator exerts a dominant cognitive influence determining certain functions (e.g. a motor function such as moving a limb).

Targeted individuals are tortured into silence, while phenomena such as *Global Hum*[27] *hearing,* which affects 4% of the world's population, may indicate that the effects are

---

[27] https://www.theguardian.com/cities/2019/mar/13/what-is-the-mysterious-gl-hum-and-is-it-simply-noise-pollution

felt by a much larger population than the targeted individuals.

Given the highly advanced nature of the reported symptoms, e.g. mental manipulation, the associated *neuroweapons*, also referred to as *weapons of mass disruption*, should be considered equivalent to weapons of mass destruction in terms of national security. They are expected to be top secret, to be handled by only a few individuals in the highest military ranks, and likely to be subject to little or no parliamentary/congressional oversight

(generic reporting citing indispensable national security covert operations). This framework would override institutional controls, thus creating environments conducive to corruption.

This is a significant human rights issue with serious risks to people's health, well-being and lives.

It is also important to understand the implications, as the targeted individuals' referrals to both torture and mind manipulation may point to a future in which mind interference may be carried out on a large scale, with imperceptible nuances and pushing thinking in certain directions, for example, for political or economic interference. It is urgent to address this phenomenon."[9]

The use of such technology to control individuals raises multiple ethical, legal and security concerns. Controlling nervous activity through invasive technologies could seriously affect personal freedom and privacy, and the implications for society should be carefully assessed before implementing such solutions. Its use should also be strictly regulated to prevent abuse and unintentional manipulation of human behavior.

In 2017, the first nanomedicine for gene therapy-Kymriah (tisagenlecleucel), a treatment for certain types of leukemia-was approved by the FDA. This marked a new frontier in the use of nanoparticles not only for drug delivery, but also for advancing gene therapies, **gene editing and immunotherapy**.

Note: some state subsystems believe that if an entity modifies someone's genes, causing behavior modification, and the mRNA (message reception) of a human being, the former has the right to the freedom of the latter, the latter becoming its slave. This is no joke. You may have wondered why you only go to certain places, why you only have certain circles, and why autonomists are outcasts, ostracized by society. The war is not really over space and territory (these being the last interest because money they already have), but over souls. Except that no one has the authority in any system, subsystem or anything else to own or subjugate a soul, a human with all that he, she, it represents, for the simple fact that they did not create it. Your body, your mind, your innate rights are under the same incidence. These rights are yours alone given to you by God!

"DARPA did a couple of contracts in 2011, 2012, with the University of California on what's called **electronic telepathy: being able to monitor the brain activity of human beings at a distance and determine what they're thinking.**
And then, a second contract that involved actually developing complex signals, being able to send them into another person's brain, to literally send a message. That's where the technology is today." **Nick Begich, mind control science researcher and educator.**
" In 2009, an article in the famous Frontline publication reported that the Defense Advanced Research Projects Agency (DARPA), which pioneered the internet in the 1960s, had budgeted $4 million to launch a program called

Silent Talk, project aimed to *enable user-to-user communication on the battlefield without the use of vocalized speech by analyzing neural signals*:

Before being vocalized, speech exists as word-specific neural signals in the mind. DARPA wants to develop a technology that can detect these pre-speech signals, analyze them, and then deliver the utterance to the intended speaker. DARPA plans to use EEG to read brain waves. It's a technique they are also testing in a project to design mind reading binoculars that could alert soldiers to threats faster than the conscious mind can process them.

The project has three major goals, according to DARPA. First, it attempts to match a person's EEG (encephalogram) patterns with their individual words. Then, see if those patterns are generalizable - if everyone has similar patterns. Finally, *to build a pre-prototype that can be used in the field, which decodes the signal and transmits over a limited range.*

This program comes after the military awarded a team from the University of California $4 million to explore *synthetic telepathy.*"

"I can disrupt an individual at the cellular and system level, and I can disrupt individuals on a variety of levels, from individuals to an entire social stratum, target a specific person, change or eliminate that person with very little attribution *(responsibility)* of blame or trace and you can get rid of any blame. Clearly, one of the things we can also do is transcranial neuromodulation, the idea of going through the skull to modulate the activity of brain nodes and network activity to implant certain brain interfaces become machine. These are many of the DARPA programs you may be hearing about now.

Probably the most notorious one is something called the N3 program, which is the noninvasive neurosurgical neuromodulation program... The idea here is to put minimally sized electrodes into a network in a brain with minimal intervention to be able to read and write brain function in real time, remotely.

And by affecting the way the brain is built and the way it works, you get a kinetic and non-kinetic change in attitudes, beliefs, thoughts, emotions. Look at the power that the tools of understanding, the techniques, the brain sciences."

" And we can make materials that have discrete properties that can be controlled by virtue of their bioengineering and their physical chemistry to automatically aggregate, to be able to aggregate in certain areas based on their biological and chemical sensitivity.

But now we're going one step further. Most recently, just a few weeks ago, it was announced that nanomaterials can be aerosolized. And we're taking it a step further, they can create small nanoscale controllable robotic units and these two can be aerosolized to create a nano swarm of biopenetrable materials that you can't see, that can penetrate all but the most robust biochemical filters and that are capable of integrating through a variety of membranes, mucous membranes, anywhere, in the mouth, nose, ears, eyes, can then be absorbed into the vascular system to create *agglomeration*.

It can affect the vascular system of the brain or diffuse directly into the brain space, and they can be weaponized."

Dr. James Giordano DARPA DARPA Neurologist/Weapons Expert-Presentation at the Modern War Institute

"A cybernetics researcher in England has developed an implantable microchip called *The Soul Catcher*. Its purpose is to record the body's electrical signals throughout a person's lifetime. This means every thought and every heartbeat will be electronically stored. Sources say many civilian researchers are unaware that a much larger wireless version is already operational. However, if neural link programs are not just recordings, a better name would be *The Soul Thief*, which turns humans into robots. This is properly part of the military system called S.A.T.A.N. Potentially millions of souls can be cataloged and *saved*. They *love* their religious metaphors in the Department of Defense/DoD." **R. Duncan, *Project: Soul Catcher***

Chris Winter of British Telecom's Artificial Life team predicted in 1996 that within three decades it would be possible to make other people's lives easier by rendering their experiences on a computer. [...] By combining this information with a record of people's genes, we could recreate a person physically, emotionally and spiritually."

[...] It might be possible to enhance a newborn baby with the experiences of a lifetime by giving it the *Soul Catcher* 2025 chip of a deceased person. [...[Dr. Winter said he takes Soul Catcher 2025 very seriously. Serious predictions by Ian Pearson (cyberneticist, mathematician, physicist), head of British Telecom's futurology unit.

N.B. It's called this way because it should be commercialized in 2025. The authors hope that by mentioning this chip and publishing the book in 2025, they are not indirectly participating in any of their own plans, or bringing any benefit to this project of theirs, whatever it may be.

"If we look at the timescales realistically, we expect that by 2050 we will be downloading our minds into a machine [...] If you are rich enough, then by 2050 is feasible. If you are poor, you will probably have to wait until 2075 or 2080, when it will become routine. We are very serious about this."

"It is possible to realize a conscious computer with superhuman intelligence before 2020. It would definitely have emotions."

We are all already in a databank. But the question is in which one? Whose bank precisely? And for what purpose exactly...?

"I have come to see what they have been working for, and the enormous ramifications for the whole social order, a new world order of people controlled electronically without their knowledge and consent." - quote from a warning.

Coming back.

The link between nanoparticles and devices.

Some sources claim that these devices could be used with nanoparticles in a range of applications combining the advantages of targeted ultrasound with the special properties of nanoscale materials.

But it is also through these technologies that many targeted individuals live a real ordeal every day. Mind and emotion control through sound and nanoparticles has some of the effects mentioned below.

Emotional manipulation through sound: Sounds, especially ultrasound, have a significant effect on people's emotional state. For example, certain acoustic frequencies can induce states of anxiety, stress, fear or even relaxation. When these technologies are combined with **nanoparticles**, the effect can be amplified. Nanoparticles could be used to carry ultrasound waves or to create an **auditory perception-altering** effect, allowing sounds to reach their intended target, such as the brain, and influence an individual's emotional states in a more effective and harder-to-detect way.

Manipulating decisions and choices: Technology of this type, if combined with nanoparticles that could be inhaled or absorbed through the skin, could allow subtle changes in an individual's perception.

Nanoparticles could interact with the nervous system to amplify **confusion** or **suggestibility** effects, making the person more susceptible to external influences, such as subliminal messages or acoustic signals that induce a state of psychological vulnerability. Thus, an individual's ability to make autonomous decisions may be disrupted without being aware of the source of the influence.

Technology and behavioral control. There are emerging theories in neurotechnological research suggesting that psychological stimulation through **targeted ultrasound** and nanoparticles could influence an individual's behaviors or thoughts at a distance.

Nanoparticles, having the ability to interact directly with the nervous system or carry acoustic signals to the brain, can amplify the effect of sound waves on the human psyche, leading to subtle **behavioral manipulation.** Although there is not yet clear evidence of the full effectiveness of these techniques, research suggests considerable potential in indirectly manipulating through the combination of acoustic and nanotechnologies.

π

War on the souls

"Psychological warfare," had been around for centuries when it became a *discovery of* World War II.

By 1964, the use of occult themes and rituals became an accepted part of psychological warfare planning. The Office of Special Operations Research at the American University "prepared a paper at the request of the U.S. Army on *Witchcraft, Magic, and Other Psychological Phenomena and Their Implications for Military and Paramilitary Operations in Congo.*"

The paper was written by James R. Price and Paul Jureidini.

Psychological warfare studies in Africa have been supported by the *Human Ecology Fund*, an organization that has been a front for the CIA's MK ULTRA program[28]."

"Some of the people involved were the same Nazis who years later escaped to the United States as part of Operation Paperclip. The relationship between occult Nazis should not surprise anyone who understands that

---

[28] *Science of Coercion: Communication Research and Psychological Warfare 1945-1960*, Christopher Simpson, Oxford University Press, NY 1994.

the highest-ranking Nazis were contaminated by the false paganism and occultism of *the Thule Gessellschaft/Thule Society*, which was absorbed into the SS with trumpets and runic chanting.

Peter Levenda in *Sinister Force* highlights the core of their practices:

"The magic was there when MK-ULTRA began its search for the paranormal and interviewed witches and wizards in America and beyond. Ceremonial magic starts from the basic premise that is sometimes phrased as the hermetic axion *As above, so below*, a simple phrase with sinister implications.

Magicians believe that there are connections and links between perceived phenomena and that to act on one side of the link is to cause a change to occur on the other side. Magicians operate in the world of non-locality, a world in which a force can be an object, a wave can be a particle (the two slits experiment) and everything is in communication with everything else."[29]

The religious and mystical dimension of the Tavistock Institute's history is central to any study of the US

---

[29] This is an excerpt from Daniel Estulin's book, *Tavistock, Institute, Social Engineering the Masses.* Redacted, interpreted and translated, but kept largely the same, because it captures it so well

government's post-war interests in how psychology and parapsychology could benefit intelligence agencies. Tavistock and the Cabala scientists, were the first to introduce paranormal abilities into military applications, being the first to develop chemicals that would stimulate psychic abilities.

This cabal included people, such as Dr. Sudney Gottlieb, the CIA's chief of staff for technical services, with obscure ties to both Operation Paperclip on the one hand and the Kennedy assassination on the other.

As Peter Levenda explains in *Sinister Forces*" a sticky fog of occultists, misguided bishops, American secret services and Nazi scientists swirled around the Kennedy assassination. All were within a handshake or two of JFK's alleged assassin, Lee Harvey Oswald.

They were all talking to ghosts, practicing magic rituals, holding hands around the Ouija board, or sacrificing chickens in New Orleans apartments. And in some cases, they were also members of America's ruling elite, the richest and most well-connected families in the country."

The CIA was not the first organization faced with the task of probing the human mind. Operations *Bluebird, Artichoke* and *MK-ULTRA*, the brainwashing operations, were designed to respond to similar practices by the Soviet Union, China and others. The show-trials of Cardinal Mindszenty[30] in Hungary were further evidence to the communists that they had succeeded in developing a technique to alter the consciousness of their political prisoners; American soldiers returning from Korean prisons was another example.

The fact that there might be a mysterious Eastern method of *messing with people's minds* both frightened and excited the CIA.

To find out as much as possible as quickly as possible, they commissioned psychiatrists, scientists and medical professionals to find out how the mind and especially memory works.

In doing so, they discovered occult practices, demonstrations of psychic abilities and mind control techniques specific to yogis, shamans and witch doctors. Clearly, this was an area of mind control worth pursuing,

---

[30] The show trials of Hungary's Cardinal Mindszenty
Cardinal Mindszenty was charged and tried for conspiracy, treason and espionage in the service of Western capitalists. The Cardinal was detained at the secret police headquarters at 60 Andrassy Avenue, which today houses the House of Terror, a museum dedicated to Hungary's dictatorial regimes. Mindszenty was beaten and tortured almost constantly for a month before he gave in and agreed to appear in a show trial in which he admitted all the charges against him.

and it spawned some of the strangest projects ever funded by the US government. It was a combination of the work of Lewin, Trist and Rees at Tavistock that led to these drugs, spiritual techniques, violence, in other words a black box of consciousness.

In this sense, Tavistock, the world's first brainwashing institute, unwittingly or knowingly followed in the footsteps of magicians, sorcerers and cultists the world over. However, there was a difference.

Principal Tavistock, Brigadier General John Rawlings Rees, Lewin, Trist or Adorno had the precise task of opening the mind for quick and easy manipulation, not to promote natural spiritual or psychic integration, or what Jung calls individuation.

Their job was to create assassins, turn agents, interrogate prisoners, get manipulation, and manipulate the conscience. Saving souls was for priests.

And since without meaning, there is no context for experience, there is no way to integrate matter into one's psychological structure without giving it meaning. [31]

---

[31] Excerpt from the book *Tavistock Instituye: Social Engineering of the Masses,* D.Estulin

In July, 1980, a major international conference was held in Toronto, Canada, under the auspices of *the First Global Conference on the Future*, attended by 4,000 social engineers, cybernetic experts and futurists from all think tanks. The conference was held under the leadership of the billionaire president of the Tavistock Institute, who set the theme:

"This conference will become a springboard for this important action to take place in the 1980s."

The agenda of the 1980 meeting mentioned above included the following:

•The women's liberation movement.

•The Consciousness of people of color, racial mixing, removing taboos against mixed marriages proposed by anthropologist Margaret Meade and Gregory Bateson of Tavistock.

•It was decided at this meeting to launch an aggressive program to portray *the colored races* as superior to the white people of Western civilization.

Out of this forum came Oprah Winfrey and a number of black people who were selected and trained for their role in portraying mixed races as superior to whites.

This could also be seen in movies, where stars of color suddenly proliferated until they became household names. This has also been seen when a person of color has been placed in the role of a high position of authority over whites, such as a judge, or a district head of the FBI and military, CEOs of large corporations, etc.

•Youth rebellion against the imagined evils of society.

•The emerging interest in corporate social responsibility businesses

•The generation gap, which implies a change of paradigm

•Experimentation with new family structures and interpersonal relationships in which homosexuality and lesbianism have become normalized

•The rise of fake conservation/ecology movements such as Greenpeace

•A growing interest in Eastern religious and philosophical perspectives

•A renewed interest in fundamentalist Christianity

•Trade unions emphasize quality of working environment

•An increased interest in meditation and other spiritual subjects, Kabala was to replace Christian culture and special people were chosen to teach and spread Kabala. The first disciples chosen were Shirley McLean, Roseanne Barr and later Madonna and Demi Moore.

- The growing importance of "self-realization" processes
- The reinvention of hip-hop and rap music by groups like Ice Cube
- A new form of language in which English is so mutilated as to be unintelligible. It will be used by newsreaders at prime time.

These disparate trends signify the emergence of a climate of social upheaval and profound changes, as a new image of the human being began to take hold, bringing with it radical changes in Western civilization.

A *leaderless* but powerful network, the *invisible army* chosen from the beginning to work to bring unacceptable change to the United States.

Its rank-and-file members were *the shock troops* that radicalized all forms of the norm. Among the *Olympians,* this network was known as the *Aquarian Conspiracy* or the *Age of Aquarius,* and its adherents would come to be known as the *shock troops.*

Above this tight-knit group of social psychologists, pollsters and media manipulators presides an elite of *powerful Olympian* patrons, *the Committee of 300.*

In the circles of the minions, it is known that this group controls everything in the world except Russia and lately China.

It plans and implements long-term strategies in a comprehensive, disciplined and unified manner.

It commands more than 400 of the top Fortune 500 companies in the U.S., with interconnected connections, that extend into every facet of government, commerce, banking, foreign policy, intelligence agencies, and military institutions.

It absorbed every other *power group* in previous US history. Rothschild, Morgan, the Rockefeller group, the eastern liberal establishment epitomized by the Perkins, Cabot, Lodge families, the cream of the old East Indian opium trade that generated billions of dollars.

Its hierarchy comprises the old families descended from the British East India Company, with its vast fortunes derived from the opium trade, which is run from the top down, including European royalty, among others." [32]

π

[32] Excerpt from *the* book *The Tavistock Institute of Human Relations - The Tavistock Institute of Human Relations,* Dr. John Coleman

EMPs and their effect on UFOs

Over the last two decades, various research has been carried out to study the effects of intensive electromagnetic fields on electrical equipment and how to counteract them. To this end, electromagnetic pulse simulators have been developed, which generate short, intense pulses that mainly affect the area around the simulator.

These simulators can emit High Power Microwave (HPM) pulses, which mimic the effects of non-ionized rays produced after an atomic explosion and can disrupt electrical circuits, affecting computers, technical devices and communication systems.

As part of the *Star Wars* program and research into non lethal weapons, electromagnetic pulse weapons have been developed. They are used to disrupt or destroy electronic equipment and have the ability to stop airplanes or other vehicles within their range causing electronic malfunctions. The 1989 simulator tests in Chesapeake Bay were accompanied by mysterious incidents.

Residents in the area have noticed an increase in the number of black military helicopters, including Chinook models, and several witnesses have reported sightings of

UFOs. The sightings are suspected to be linked to secret military tests.

A project known as EMPRESS-Electromagnetic Pulse Radiation Environment Simulator for Ships-has been carried out by the US Navy, involving the testing of electromagnetic pulses on a ship.

During these tests, anomalies were observed and witnesses reported the presence of UFOs near the test area.

Chris Terraneau, who was involved between 1987 and 1989 in building a weapon system based on high-performance electromagnetic pulses (HPM), explained that these weapons work by using a Marx generator to produce voltage and electronic pulses, which are then converted into microwaves by a Magnetron device. Tests show that such weapons can easily destroy electronic equipment, including computers and military devices. After leaving the research team, Terraneau learned that HPM research continued under a higher degree of secrecy and funding.

In November 1993, Dr. John Alexander[33] organized a conference at Johns Hopkins University on electromagnetic

---

[33] Dr. John Alexander is well known in the field of non-lethal weapons research and research related to advanced technologies, including electromagnetic weapons. He has been involved in military research and has worked for various government agencies.

weapons, attended by leaders of the high-tech weapons industry, with Dr. Edward Teller as guest host.

The conference discussed both energy weapons used against humans and those that can be directed against equipment, airplanes and vehicles. Among the technologies mentioned were high-frequency microwave pulse weapons and electromagnetic pulse (EMP) weapons, which can disrupt electrical circuits, endangering airplanes and vehicles.

Dr. John Alexander, in his spare time, was interested in exploring paranormal phenomena and UFOs. In an article in *Aviation Week & Space Technology* magazine on January 24, 1993, Dr. Alexander suggested that antimatter weapons were being developed in the US. There has been particular interest in EMP weapons because they are very effective for Special Forces missions, operating quickly and efficiently without being visible. These weapons could, in theory, also be used against UFOs, as these flying objects could ionize the air around them[34] , indicating that their propulsion could depend on electric currents and magnetic fields.

---

[34] Hypothetically, these weapons could also be used against UFOs. In the paper *UFO-Nahbegegnungen/Close encounters* it was shown that UFOs can ionize the air around them. This is an indication that the propulsion UFOs rely on electric currents and magnetic fields

Thus, electromagnetic pulses produced by HPM and PEM weapons could disrupt or override the electrical systems of UFOs.

There are suspicions that EMP (electromagnetic pulse) weapons may be used to *attack* UFOs.

But why are they so interested in attacking them? Would those piloting those unidentified objects somehow help the human race? Do they really think they can shoot one down? In our humble opinion the major interest most likely is to capture one for reasons known to them only.

The EMPRESS[35] tests, as well as UFO-related research, suggest that the military could use these weapons to combat possible UFO *intrusions* (?), especially since some UFOs may interact with the electromagnetic fields produced by these weapons. Although there is no direct evidence, research from test sites such as Gulf Breeze in Florida suggests a link between UFO sightings and the military's electromagnetic pulse experiments.

Leah Haley, a person who claims to have been abducted by both UFOs and armed forces, recalls a strange experience

---

[35] **J.M. Nelson, CH.S.J ones, L.A. Poston**, *USS Anzio EMPRESS II trial*, March 2009 *Naval Engineers Journal* 108(3):315 - 333 DOI:10.1111/j.1559-3584.1996.tb01569.

where she was examined aboard a UFO and later saw intense military activity. Investigating the area where she believed the incident occurred, Haley and MUFON researchers discovered an antenna and equipment that appeared to be electromagnetic weapons. At the same time, reports in the military press suggest that the military is testing such weapons and using them to shoot down airplanes, which reinforces the above hypothesis.

This research and related events could suggest that the US military is developing and testing weapons that use electromagnetic pulses to counter possible *extraterrestrial threat*[36].

An EMP/electromagnetic pulse can also be produced from non-nuclear sources, such as electromagnetic bombs, or E-bombs. High altitude nuclear detonations and electromagnetic bombs can generate an EMP with the potential to damage or destroy electronic devices over large areas.

An EMP is characterized by a strong energy pulse, usually very short in duration (on the order of nanoseconds or microseconds).

---

[36] *The authors of the book do not perceive the extraterrestrial life, if such would exist, as being a threat.*

Electricity supply systems would also be at risk of power surges from such weapons.

A non-nuclear EMP (electromagnetic pulse) is produced by devices that generate intense electromagnetic fields without using nuclear reactions. These devices typically involve rapidly discharging electricity into a coil or antenna, creating a short-lived electromagnetic pulse capable of damaging or disrupting electronic circuits in a localized area.

Why are MEPs important?

On NATO's website[37] you will find the following reported: "Military operations in all environments use the electromagnetic spectrum to create effects that support military objectives. As part of the battlefield, NATO forces conduct electromagnetic operations in the electromagnetic environment.

Electromagnetic operations involve activities that exploit the electromagnetic environment to support or enhance NATO operations and to impede a potential adversary's ability to do the same.

---

[37] North Atlantic Treaty Organization NATO, Electromagnetic Warfare/NATO- Topic: Electromagnetic Warfare

[...] Electromagnetic Warfare activities represent military actions that exploit electromagnetic energy to provide situational awareness and create offensive and defensive effects.

From attacks on radar systems, to jamming communications and navigation systems, to electronic masking, probes, reconnaissance and intelligence gathering, electromagnetic warfare can be applied in all operational domains - air, land, sea, space and cyber. It is therefore essential that NATO remains ready and able to counter the use of EW[38] by any potential adversary.

Electromagnetic warfare should not be confused with cyber warfare and its capabilities. In general, cyber operations use various hacking techniques to infiltrate and disrupt a target's computer systems in order to gain information or degrade its capabilities.

Electromagnetic warfare uses directed energy to disrupt access to the electromagnetic spectrum, blocking signals between technologies and rendering them inoperable.

Of course, by interfering with information infrastructure, electromagnetic warfare can affect cyber operations.

---

[38] Electromagnetic Warfare

Electromagnetic warfare was previously referred to as *electronic warfare* by NATO, and the two terms are often used interchangeably. The term electromagnetic warfare is now preferred, to emphasize the importance of the electromagnetic spectrum in EW-electromagnetic warfare."[39]

π

[39] North Atlantic Treaty Organization NATO, Electromagnetic Warfare/NATO- Topic: Electromagnetic Electromagnetic Warfare

Synthetic telepathy - a brief history

Voice to skull (V2K) telepathy, or *voice to brain/skull* or *pulsed microwave technology* as it is called in scientific circles, has been researched and described by several scientists and amateurs.

Voice-to-skull telepathy is the communication between a human mind and a host mind or synthetic intelligence by means of weapons or other devices that generally use directed energy.

In the paper *Synthetic Telepathy and the First Mind Wars,* c2001, presented at the *Conference on Consciousness Technologies*, July 19-21, 2001, Saturday, July 20, 2001, in Sisters, OR, Richard Alan Miller describes a number of studies and methods, devices discovered and used in mind manipulation.

During this conference in **2001**, Mr. Miller described the technology that transmits information via microwaves. This, and other uses of it, will be described below.

In 1961, Allen Frey, an independent biophysicist and psychologist, reported in his study[40] that humans can hear

---

[40] *Human auditory system auditory response to modulated electromagnetic energy* Allan H. Frey 01 Jul 1962, Journal of Applied Physiology https://doi.org/10.1152/jappl.1962.17.4.689

microwave emissions[41] . Most scientists in the United States dismissed this finding by labeling it as the result of background noise.

James C. Linn gave a more detailed description of Frey's experiment, explaining technically how this phenomenon was observed.

"Frey found that human subjects exposed to microwave emissions between 1310 MHz and 2982 MHz with average power densities between 0.4 and 2 mW/cm^2 perceived auditory sensations described as a buzzing or knocks.

These sensations occurred instantaneously, even at signal intensities well below the threshold that would cause obvious biological damage, and the source of the sensation appeared to come from inside or near the back of the head."

---

[41] Microwaves are very high-frequency electromagnetic (radiation) waves propagating at the speed of light. Typical applications: thermal effects applications, telecommunications, electronic surveillance, radiolocation and remote sensing, microwave spectroscopy, defectoscopy, medical investigations, power microwaves (thermo-microwave).
Microwaves - electromagnetic waves - whose wavelength is comparable to the dimensions of the propagation space: ultrashort-wave (UHF - so called FM radio stations)
TV waves inside an apartment room, radio waves for GSM telephony, national or continental electricity transmission network.
Microwaves generally mean electromagnetic waves with frequencies in the range 0.3÷300GHz, i.e. wavelengths in the range 1m÷1mm.

The technology described above is the transmission of voice to the skull (or other sounds to the skull) via microwaves, and was discovered during World War II by the radiolocation technicians who found that they could hear the sound generated by the pulses transmitted by the radar equipment they were working with.

This phenomenon has been extensively studied by Dr. Allan Frey (Willow Grove, 1965), whose research has been published in several reference books.

Dr. Frey found that individual microwave pulses could be audibly perceived by some people as pops/cracks or clicks, while a continuous series of uniform pulses could be heard as a hum, without the need for any type of classical receiver. Dr. Frey found that over a wide range of frequencies, even at values much lower than the frequencies characteristic of microwaves, such as 125 MHz, this effect of *microwaves hearing* is generated when the correct combinations of power and pulse width are used.

These detailed observations have been derived from unclassified studies, which have led to the identification of the most effective frequencies and impulse characteristics that *facilitate* this auditory phenomenon.

Very important, when discussing **electronic mind control**, is the fact that the peak pulse power required to produce this effect is small, namely about 0.3-watt cm² of skull surface. This power level is only applied or required for a very short interval of each pulse cycle.

For example, 0.3 watt/cm² is equivalent to the power emitted by a 250-watt heating lamp at a distance of one meter. This is a small amount of energy.

When considering that the pulse series is off (no signal) for most of each cycle, the average signal strength is extremely low and almost impossible to detect. This is the concept of *peak* wave used in radio detection and other forms of military communication.

In terms of transmission technology, the frequencies that act as the carrier waves of the voice to the skull are not simple frequencies, such as those used for television or cell phones, but are wide ranges or bands of frequencies.

To reduce interference and detectability of the signals, a technology called broad spectrum is used, whereby the carrier frequencies *bounce* continuously within a specified frequency band. Without a receiver that *knows* this frequency *hopping* program in advance, as with other forms of encryption, there is virtually no chance of receiving or detecting a coherent and readable signal, some experts say. This is an encryption mechanism, and the modulated signals appear as *noise* on detection devices such as spectrum analyzers, which are equipment used to measure and analyze electromagnetic signals.

In the 1974 experiment conducted by Dr. Joseph C. Sharp and Mark Grove performed the first direct voice transmission to the skull using Frey-type audible Frey pulses at the Walter Reed Army Institute of Research[42]

These were transmitted every time the voice wave passed through the zero axes of the signal, a technique that can be reproduced by amateur radio operators who build their own equipment.

The reported sensation is similar to a buzzing, clicking or hissing sound that seems to come from inside or even behind the head/brain.

The phenomenon occurs at densities as low as microwatts per square centimeter, with carrier frequencies between 0.3-3.0 GHz. With the appropriate choice of pulse characteristics, clear speech messages can be obtained.

---

[42] *Walter Reed Army Institute of Research* is the largest biomedical research center administered by the US Department of Defense/DoD.

Dr. James Lin of Wayne State University has written a paper entitled *Auditory Effects of Microwaves and their Applications*, which explores the possible physiological mechanisms underlying this phenomenon. Lin also discussed the possibility that people who are deaf or have partial hearing loss may be able to perceive pulsed microwave signals as tones or clicks if speech signals are modulated correctly. Lin mentions Sharp and Grove's experiment and comments: "The ability to communicate directly with people via microwaves is clearly not limited to the field of therapeutic medicine".

In 1975, researcher A. W. Guy stated that "one of the most widely observed and accepted biological effects of medium power electromagnetic radiation is the auditory sensation evoked in man when exposed to pulsed microwaves (discontinuously transmitted microwaves)".

He concluded that, at frequencies at which the auditory effect can be easily detected, microwaves penetrate deep into the tissues of the head, causing a rapid thermal[43] expansion that produces stresses in brain tissue.

---

[43] In the context, reference is made to the effect of microwaves on brain tissue. The rapid thermal expansion mentioned refers to the fact that electromagnetic radiation can generate localized heating of the tissue, which causes it to expand microscopically. This expansion, at the cellular level, can create mechanical stress in brain tissue, leading to the sensations described.

An acoustic stress wave is then transmitted through the skull to the cochlea[44] , and from there, it proceeds in the same way as in conventional hearing. It is evident that receiverless radio technology has not been sufficiently publicized or explained due to national security concerns.

Today, sources claim that the ability to transmit voices directly into a target's head using microwaves is known within the Pentagon as *synthetic telepathy*.

According to Dr. Robert Becker, synthetic telepathy has applications in covert operations designed to psychologically disrupt a target by inducing auditory hallucinations, or to transmit undetected instructions to a programmed agent or assassin.

The technology may have contributed to the deaths of 25 defense scientists employed by Marconi Underwater and

---

[44] An acoustic wave, (as it appears in the original text), is transmitted through the skull to the cochlea (the part of the inner ear responsible for sound perception). The process described assumes that the rapid thermal expansion of brain tissue caused by microwaves generates a mechanical vibration (called an acoustic stress wave), which propagates through the internal structures of the head. In more detail, the acoustic wave is created when electromagnetic radiation (microwaves) is absorbed by brain tissue, causing it to dilate rapidly at the microscopic level. This rapid expansion generates mechanical stresses that form an acoustic wave that propagates through the skull, similar to the way sound travels through the air or other media. Once the wave reaches the cochlea, it is perceived by the auditory system as if it were created by external sound sources. In this way, the sound wave is transmitted mechanically, by vibration, from the brain tissue to the internal auditory structures, without the need for a radio receiver in the classical sense.

Defense Systems, Easems and GEC. Most of them were working on highly sensitive electronic warfare programs for NATO, including in the area of strategic defense strategies.

Coming back.

It is strange how biblical prophecy, science, military technology and sociology seem to come together and converge at this important point in time in the development of our species.

"We tried to adapt evil as people perceive it, to create weaponry that attacks the information systems of the brain and the body. We didn't know at the time what we were doing. I regret what I did." Former DARPA employee and scientist.

"In some cases, *the psychic warrior* gives up his soul while *maintaining* close frequency oscillations (heterodyning-heterodyning[45]) with a host mind, and usually with an unwanted host. Hence *the inspiration* for the book *Project: Soul Catcher*.

---

[45] Heterodyne is an electronic generator used to produce high-frequency oscillations or fitting used in radio engineering to produce beats by interference of two oscillations of very close frequencies.

The patterns of information, which they invent, are significantly altered through the collective mind configuration, one mind trying to dominate another. A man would have to hate his soul very much to accept having his soul altered so much."

Robert Duncan, *Project* **book***: Soul Catcher.*

*

Acoustic Heterodyne-Audio Spotlight[46]

It can be used in two main ways:

-as directed sound, to create a private listening space for a particular

-as projected sound, in which sound is projected towards a distant object, creating an audio image.

This audio image is similar to a projected speaker and the sound seems to come directly from the projection, similar to light.

Audio Spotlight consists of a thin, circular array of transducers and a specially designed signal processor and amplifier. The transducer is thin, odorless and lightweight,

---

46
https://www.roi.ru/tmp/attachments/718817/synthetictelepathyandt heearlymindwars--kopiia1509733759.pdf

and the signal processor and amplifier are integrated into a unit similar in size to a traditional audio amplifier.

OK! And why do I need to know that? Read on.

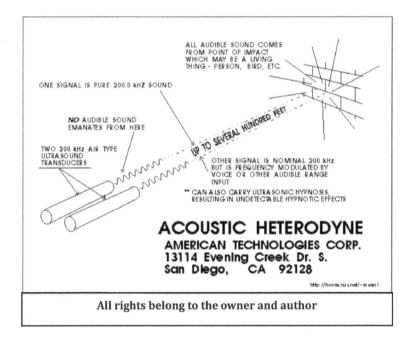

ALL AUDIBLE SOUND COMES FROM POINT OF IMPACT WHICH MAY BE A LIVING THING - PERSON, BIRD, ETC.

ONE SIGNAL IS PURE 200.0 kHZ SOUND

NO AUDIBLE SOUND EMANATES FROM HERE

TWO 200 kHz AIR TYPE ULTRA SOUND TRANSDUCERS

UP TO SEVERAL HUNDRED FEET

OTHER SIGNAL IS NOMINAL 200 kHz BUT IS FREQUENCY MODULATED BY VOICE OR OTHER AUDIBLE RANGE INPUT

** CAN ALSO CARRY ULTRASONIC HYPNOSIS, RESULTING IN UNDETECTABLE HYPNOTIC EFFECTS

ACOUSTIC HETERODYNE
AMERICAN TECHNOLOGIES CORP.
13114 Evening Creek Dr. S.
San Diego,   CA   92128

http://home.nasnet/~raven1

The use of these technologies for remote targeting purposes or to direct sound to specific individuals or groups is a delicate and sensitive ethical and legal issue.

In theory, such devices could be used to project sound in a particular direction, such as to transmit messages or sounds directly to an individual or group of people without disturbing others nearby.

This principle could be utilized in a way that could, in principle, target individuals remotely. That is, only one person or a specific few in a group could hear those messages.

Below you can read about potential uses, as exemplified by some sources, in the context of this technology being used against targeted individuals.

Directed noise discomfort

These technologies could be used to produce highly disturbing or annoying sounds (such as frequent or irritating noises) directed only at the target individuals.

For example, high-frequency ultrasound can be very unpleasant or uncomfortable, but is not perceived by most people unless it is directed at a specific area or person.

Direct communication and confidentiality

It could be used to send audible messages or commands directed exclusively to a target person, for example in a security or control situation, without that person knowing who is sending the message.

Crowd control

For crowd control or dissuasion purposes, this technology could be used to direct sound at individuals or groups to create confusion or discomfort, without affecting the whole area or leaving visible traces. In theory, it could be used in a similar way to other acoustic crowd dispersal devices (e.g. by generating loud noises to disorient or intimidate).

Hyper directivity

The directivity of an acoustic wave is proportional to the ratio between the diameter of the transducer and the wavelength of the sound. Such devices can generate small ultrasonic waves that form a very narrow beam even in a small transducer. This maintains a uniform directivity over the entire audible frequency spectrum compared to traditional loudspeakers, which have a much wider directivity.

From here to the transmission of such noises, messages using drones was just a close step. Keep in mind this device was presented at the conference in 2001, already existing and tested.

π

A certain overseas agency recruits mostly from secret societies, fraternities and sororities, all kinds of clubs, psychosects, army, navy, making use of the induced arrogance and importance of the members belonging to these societies, institutions, using the *method of feeding their vanity*. Thus, the agency easily controls recruits in order for them to accomplish certain tasks that support the use of weapons of mass control. Recruits can play the role of boyfriends, candidates, commissioners in businesses, political parties and so on. At times they can interpret the role of a targeted individual. In general, any role that suits the agency best, making them actors for the necessary occasion.

*

Excerpt from an interview with an interviewee who was subjected to torture with a S.A.T.A.N. weapon.

"They didn't seem to hide what they were doing. For several months they would induce pain, which they would inform about and measure the level of pain. They said some tortures hurt more when the person knew what was coming. They usually ran three new types of pain every day. Then the experiments changed. They would transmit new pains and ask me what to name them so they could put them in their database. Later they boasted that they could turn me into an alcoholic, drug addict, smoker, psychopath, or even a church lady, depending on how they thought it would serve the success of their project.

Simulated rape and sexual humiliation techniques:

A sweet young Asian woman described her ordeal.

<<I was lying in bed after a day of psychological abuse coupled with physical pain. The pulsating tinnitus like a phasing sound had become silent so that later I could hear a man's voice speaking to me. Then I felt him above me like a ghost. Then he raped me again and again, telling me there was no stopping him. I could feel him masturbating. It's hard to describe. >>

You don't have to be too creative to figure out how to do this trick. It's a pretty standard practice during brainwashing, and are practiced for the purpose of creating alternate personalities by violating the mind and body, or both. Welcome to the United States of America! We're not allowed to talk about it," describes R. **Duncan in the book *Project: Soul catcher***

Unfortunately, the psychology industry has created a term for people like this woman: *false memory syndrome*. This is just a play on words and a farce for understanding an experience like this. The memories are real and created in real time. They are experiences of physical events induced by weapons using directed energy that the brain cannot differentiate from physical reality *(on a sidenote, it can)* because by stimulating centers in the brain the symptoms are registered as real. Only the person concerned knows they are not real.

Note: the brain can make up the difference, but requires training an attention.

Duncan describes these *acts* as, of course, real and intentional mental crimes. Some subjects of DoD/CIA experiments even believe they were real, not just *ghosts*, as this woman did. In the past, the CIA has used alien masks during physical extraditions to deflect hatred against them. In context some people have wondered why aliens have traveled across the galaxy to Earth, only to anal probe the subjects of their abduction. This is just a standard way of inducing trauma that predisposes the individual to behavioral changes." **Robert Duncan,** *Project: Soul Catcher*

π

2017-Bucharest

Iiris was in the room where the integrative psychotherapy module was taking place, when she felt an intense telepathic alertness and the need to go outside. She was in the middle of the module and couldn't get out then because an exercise was being taking act and the silence in the classroom was unbearable. She had connected to that impulse and visualized someone reaching into her purse and taking something from there. She saw the door keys. All purses and cell phones and personal belongings were left by the trainees at the entrance in a neat and protected place.

Iiris hadn't gone out to check in that right moment, she told herself it was just a momentary perception and couldn't believe it was true.

At the break he checked her bag and looking carefully at the bundle of keys she realized that the key from the bottom knob of the door was missing.

She blinked in disbelief. She looked again as if expecting it to reappear. No, it didn't reappear. She was shocked. She wanted to call the police and personally check the camera, but it was not positioned to capture images in that angle but towards the entrance. She looked at the secretary and noticed a faltering nonverbal language. She assessed the situation and preferred to go further to see where exactly this situation was leading. She intuitively perceived that it was more than that.

I'll call the owner, she thought to herself.

Ah, the owner went to America! I have to call him to ask if he has a spare key somewhere. He'd said something about a brother," she calmed herself down, trying to look for solutions.

That same evening Iiris was due to arrive at the concert for which she had already bought two tickets. From the psychotherapy class she had left for the concert after checking with her friend what time they were to meet. She explained to her friend what had happened and asked her if it would be okay if she stayed at her place for the night until she sorted out her problem.

Meanwhile she phoned the landlord and told him what had happened. He did not seem surprised. He suggested to call his brother who lived nearby the area where the studio was located. Having obtained the latter's number, she had phoned him, told him about the situation he was in, and made sure she had his confirmation that he would come in the morning to hand over the spare key.

After the concert, at her friend's invitation, the girls headed to a pizzeria in the old town whose new owner was *a lady* of foreign origin. She spoke Romanian but at an intermediate level.

On the way, by the time she got to that pizzeria Iiris noticed a general agitation, people passing by, just loudly pronouncing certain words as if trying to warn her. Something, someone was trying to get her attention, but she didn't understand what it was. Something was going to happen. Just before she entered the pizzeria, out of nowhere a cable had suddenly short-circuited in front of her. Tension was literally and figuratively high. As she entered the pizzeria, after a pleasant conversation, *the madam* offered a pizza on the house.

The whole atmosphere was charged like a cloud about to erupt, but everyone pretended that everything was fine. Iiris could sense something was going on, but he wasn't sure exactly what. She waited to see what would come next.

A few details had been mentioned during the conversation that she didn't know what to believe and do about.

She was in the middle of some events that she didn't know why they were happening to her, what role she had in all of those events. The landlord had a as friendly an attitude as *she* could possibly have, but throughout the conversation she accompanied her with menacing and watchful eyes.

The two friends left the scene, hailed a taxi and headed to her friend's house. On the way, shortly after boarding the taxi, a verbal conflict broke out between the two out of nowhere, provoked by her friend.

The latter was accusing her out of the blue of something non-existent, and Iiris was trying to bring her back to reality, but she had the impression that something had taken control of her. She couldn't get sense into her, and at 12 o'clock at night when she arrived at the place where she was supposed to spend the night, Iiris had to call the owner's brother to ask for the spare key.

"I don't know if I have it, I need to check which bundle of keys it's in," he replied calmly as if he wasn't surprised by the phone call at that hour.

"It's 12 at night and I have nowhere to go now. I'll possibly sleep at the dump[47] if you can't come, and in the morning, I'll wait for you."

"No dump for tonight! Possibly if we don't find the key you sleep here. You can come to me and we can go together and

---

[47] Dumps are usually located at the same level with the flats in a separate room and having a separate entrance

try the keys."

Iiris was relieved to have found a solution and continued the taxi ride to the address given by the man. From there they proceeded to where the studio apartment was."

In the parking lot of the block where Iiris lived, she saw two individuals standing in front of a car with Teleorman license plate, in front of which, at the bottom, was a hastily manufactured cross.

On either side, stood the two individuals, staring at the girl. She saw a waggish grin on their faces, and turned in time to notice the same waggishness on the face of the man beside her. She returned her gaze to the two, more puzzled by the significance of what was happening, and looked through the windshield again at the two men staring at her, who were staring at her in a fixed and subdued way.

"Are they expecting someone? At this hour? Are they sending a message to someone? But to whom? They wouldn't have to! I am the Earth's peace," Iiris said using self-irony to defuse the situation. But everyone was tensed.

"I don't understand what is going on with these people lately. God forbid! At 12 o'clock at night to stand in front of the building and a car and flank it with a cross lying on the ground. They're all out of their minds! And the cross isn't just any cross. It's handmade out of some bits of newspaper or something. How bizarre! What are they trying to say? Cause I truly cannot figure it out. And not just any kind of cross...uh, the old-rite Russian one. Funny thing is, I was born in the old rite", said Iiris closing her monologue.

She had the impression that it was a form of threat that she didn't know how to interpret it and what it meant, and why she was receiving it. She was in the middle of events she didn't know what to think of.

Meanwhile he dialed the emergency number on the screen, just in case, and looked around to see if people were passing by. She had called the landlord earlier to let him know that she had found the solution to head to the studio with his brother.

They got out of the car, Iiris continuing to stare at the individuals with the cross, and maintain eye contact until they passed them and headed for the entrance. They finally went up to the 7th floor, and there the owner's brother tried every key in the bundle. Apparently, none was a fit.

Iiris began to feel irritated and began to understand why the two were downstairs and why the cross looked so disorganized, as if hastily made to serve an immediate purpose. Perhaps it was a beneficial warning and someone was trying to protect her from sleeping in the studio that night, or perhaps the other way around, sleeping in the other apartment.

Let intuition do the talking! Said to herself.

Something was telling her to stay there, in the studio. But the thoughts were insistent and at the time she didn't know that someone was actually interfering with her thoughts, causing her to ignore her intuition.

"None of them fit. We have to come back in the morning," the man said.

"Give them to me please! I want to try!"

No, forget it, I already tried them. Can't you see they don't match? Maybe it's in the other bundle I left at home," he said in a convincing tone.

"Well, you said that the other bundle contains the keys to your house, and that this one has all the keys that belong to the studio", Iiris explained logically, remembering the conversation and the moment when she suggested to take the other bundle so as not to make two trips.

Iiris, suspicious of all the things that have happened and the turn of events, told the man that she would sleep in the dumpster or cellar. She had the key to the cellar that was on the same floor and could sleep there until morning.

"No, come to my place! Where are you going to sleep here?" he said convincingly but without offering to go and get the second bundle and open the door. It was only a three minute drive.

There was something about that man that didn't inspire trust. She didn't want to go, and as events unfolded, she convinced herself that something wasn't exactly accidental. She checked the future timeline and detected no major problem, only a hidden and bizarre intent.

She really couldn't understand what were all those events about. She just sensed that something was being prepared for her. Something hidden somehow.

She thanked him for the offer, and accepted only because the floor cellar had no toilet. She asked for the address and had given it to her mother and brother in a message. She informed them of her situation, and that she was staying at Jim's place for the night. She phoned the landlord to inform him of the change of situation and was surprised when he was told that no key had been found to fit.

The two little pets in the man's apartment took an instant liking to Iiris. The dog sat comfortably on her lap, and the cat beside her while she chatted with the studio owner's brother and drank tea.

He was astonished by the fact that the animals attached to Iiris so fast and affectionate. His face expressed a mix of wonder and *a missing puzzle piece*, something changing in him. After the girl had occupied a couch on which she was to sleep that night, the animals took shelter beside her as if to protect her, Jim being surprised again by the animals' behavior.

The next day, after a short conversation and a coffee, a friend of Jim showed up. They were both bizarre. The latter was an insider of the secret military system, he would later *confess*.

He was staring at her as if he wanted to get something out of her. Iiris tried to understand what they wanted from her, but intuitively she felt safe. A safety that came from elsewhere, not from them.

At one point the owner's brother had said something about her ugliness out of nowhere in the middle of the conversation and was waiting for the girl's reaction. They both were. Iiris knew that this was the way to draw the connection channels on the personal frequency, so she looked at them for a while and amusedly answered them:

"For some I am beautiful, for some ugly, it depends on who is looking and on the intention of my interlocutor. Beauty is in the eye of the beholder, isn't it?" Iiris asked amused and rhetorically.

"But what has that statement regarding my appearance got to do with the discussion we are having?" she asked, amused, realizing the intention of the detractor in front of her.

Obviously the two were silent, and the newcomer didn't like the way things were going. The three of them went to the girl's studio to *find the right key*, and there they had an interesting discussion. Evidently, the key was on the same ring used the previous evening.

Iiris made a cup of coffee for everyone and served them some cookies, out of universal hospitality, not because they were welcome. Their energy imprint was so heavy to bear and their intention so nasty as a feel that she could stand too close too them. The discussion continued and as it did, they tried to insert negative, self-sabotaging programs, which Iiris spotted *on the fly*.

The militaryinsider asked her a question that sounded more like a statement, wanting to make sure she no longer believed in flying objects.

Iiris surprised, replied that she would believe it when she would drive one or when one *parked* in front of the balcony. She knew there was a lot of mass misinformation out there, but she didn't rule out the existence of a superior civilization that somehow makes its presence known in one way or another.

It was just that she perceived a beneficial influence and a malefic one. That's all. And no one could convince her otherwise. She was what she was.

"But why all of a sudden the UFO thing?"

Why would he want to make sure I don't believe in UFOs anymore?

Was that a threat or what? I really don't get it. Honestly, it's not a joke and I'm not being ironic. I have the right to believe what I think it's natural to believe based on the data that exists, gathered and analyzed, and I don't think anyone has the right to tell me what to think, what to accept to think. But obviously, for a piece of information to become a conviction, I need evidence", concluded Iiris looking into the eyes of the newcomer, nervousness rising like a phoenix.

"But why are you so interested in my opinion on the subject anyway? Why would care? We were talking about coffee and suddenly you changed the subject to flying objects. What's the big deal?", questioned Iiris with all sincerity.

The landlord's brother intervened with a threatening statement that Iiris did not know how to register.

To clarify, she asked him some natural but clarifying questions. He reiterated the negative program, and Iiris instantly returned it without giving him a chance to think or say anything more. It was as if a force was acting through her, and rightly so. It was protecting her from something ugly and evil. She had invited them to end the visit, as she had a long day and work to do and the situation was taking a turn that would not end well.

The woman thought about the events and how they were manipulated from the shadows. She didn't understand anything except that she was caught in a game she wasn't aware of. More than half the world knew about this insidious *game*, only she didn't. But she didn't like it and it contradicted her values. What were the motives and motivations of these people?

She carefully reviewed everything that had happened and promised herself that she would listen to her intuition more carefully as she had always done, except that lately she had a lot of unwanted influences that she didn't know how to relate to.

And no, it wasn't the Blue Beam project about the conversation she had with that suspicious individual. Their effort was too much and too big. If it was just laser projections, there wouldn't be so much effort after all.

Iiris had often seen lights in the skies of Bucharest around 2016, and had seen them again in certain areas of the country and on Ceahlău mountains, and in other countries. They were around her and she felt their beneficial presence on an *animic* (anima) level. But she did not understand what was the problem with these individuals. And then she perceived a very low vibration of them and others. She recognized this vibration in many of the future attempts of relationship coming from different parts.

*

In that one-room apartment Iiris had been in indescribable pain and discomfort. She was sure she was being subjected to a social, eugenic experiment, and data was being collected on her responses to stimuli. Both she and the few other residents in the block had similar symptoms. Iiris had started her research a long time ago, and sensed that something was definitely wrong. She wanted to find out, but her progress was slowed by the fact that her recent memory was impaired due to *subtle* interference and she had to reread much of what he had memorized in order to synthesize it. In the past she had extraordinary synthesizing capacity and a great memory. But since 2014 when she returned to the country, things have changed.

*

Sometime after the incident the landlord came to collect the rent. They talked for a while, then he left. Something summoned Iiris to catch up to see something. She changed and went downstairs quickly, intending to see if what she had perceived was true, but also to buy something from the store.

Done and done. Arriving downstairs, Iiris saw the owner of the studio apartment with his godfather, and opening the door, she was able to overhear enough of the conversation to realize that she was being monitored, though she had plenty of other evidence to prove it.

"And what did you talk about?" asked the landlord's relative. Did she say anything? How is it?" he tried to find out more.

"Well, I don't know, she said something in there about..." said the studio owner who upon hearing the door shrugged and looked back, immediately silent after seeing Iiris. The expression of his face freezed.

"But when did you get downstairs?" he asked, dumbfounded.

"This is the relative I was telling you about," the landlord whispered, surprised that Iiris had come down the stairs so fast and found her behind him. HE sensed that she had overheard the conversation, but not sure how much, his facial expression indicating that he was an informer.

"I went out to buy something," the girl replied, sensing the thought and the next question, and to give some sort of answer; she walked towards the store leaving the two behind her.

The relative worked in the secret service system.

Iiris wanted to know what was going on with her and had for some years started to study various topics ranging from paranormal phenomena to psychology, social dynamics, stalking, and their applicability to her and other people, psychiatric case histories. People who were on lists unknown to anyone, who were being harassed for reasons unknown to them, and suffering indescribable tortures. Symptoms ranged from physical to psychic, mental, or a mixture of all three. Most were monitored since childhood.

Target individuals - retrospective

After 9/11 and the birth of Homeland Security, fusion centers were set up to monitor U.S. citizens, and the U.S. Department of Justice legalized nonconsensual experiments on the public. These fusion centers employ civilians to target and harass innocent individuals, intimidate them, vandalize their property, and interfere with their daily lives. This is known as *gang stalking*.

Former high-ranking FBI agent Ted Gunderson reported in 2011 that himself and thousands of others had been targeted. FBI agent Mike German confirmed this as well. Several federal agents have reported that ordinary Americans are being targeted (including people who were simply pro-life), and that they were pressured to put more people on their watch lists in order to legitimize more federal funding.

These Homeland Security fusion centers are capable of putting any American citizen on a watch list without any reason or due process. In 2012, NSA whistleblower William Binney reported that the feds conduct comprehensive surveillance on approximately every American citizen, and target anyone they want. In 2014, Glenn Greenwald revealed the methods used to target individuals, including hacking into people's social media accounts, presenting themselves as that person, and contacting their friends and colleagues.

The UN Special Rapporteur on Torture, Niels Melzer and his team are working on a legal framework to protect humanity, suggesting a mechanism to protect against AI/AI-controlled radio frequency spectrum to protect targeted individuals from cyber-technological torture.

And it should be so, because the subversive tactics of mental torture, harassment, stalking, hacking electronic devices, interfering in personal emotional space, provoking the worsening of the quality of life to the point of complete isolation of the individual and inducing self-destructive behavior and thoughts, must stop and these people must regain their freedom in every respect.

The subversive actions to which many targeted individuals are subjected are very similar to the FBI's COINTELPRO actions, a Counter Espionage program carried out between 1956 and 1971. There is no public data on whether it continued or not, but observing the dynamics in all walks of life, the political, military, economic scene, one could logically deduce not only that it continued but, it also enriched its methods of action.

The FBI claimed that the purpose behind COINTELPRO was to *unmask, disrupt, misdirect or neutralize in other than what* were considered *subversive,* FBI field agents were trained to:

1. create a negative public image for target groups - e.g. by monitoring activists and then releasing negative personal information to the public

2. organized destruction from within, creating conflicts of all kinds, such as asking agents to exacerbate racial tensions or send anonymous letters to try to create conflict

3. create dissension between groups e.g. by spreading rumors that other groups are stealing money

4. restrict access to public resources by, for example, pressuring non-profit organizations to cut off funding or material support

5. limit the ability to organize protests e.g. by agents promoting violence against police during planning and at protests

6. restrict the ability of individuals to participate in group activities e.g. by destroying public image, false arrests, surveillance

In February, 1996, Noam Chomsky - political activist and MIT linguistics professor - spoke about the aims and targets of COINTELPRO, saying:

"COINTELPRO was a program of subversion carried out not by a few crooks, but by the national political police, the FBI, under four administrations...during the course of the program being targeted by many groups, the whole new left, the whole feminist movement, the whole movement of people of color...it was extremely broad. His actions went as far as political assassination."

COINTELPRO documents show numerous instances where the FBI's intentions to prevent and disrupt anti-Vietnam War protests were clear. Many techniques were used to accomplish this task. "These included promoting divisions among anti-war forces, encouraging persecution of socialists, and promoting violent confrontations as an alternative to peaceful mass demonstrations."

π

Target individuals - Who are they?

In the context it should be noted that an individual is a human being who is regarded as a distinct unit from other persons. According to some sources, the individual (from lat. *individuum* - that which cannot be divided), is someone singular, his wholeness being associated with his uniqueness, since no two people are identical in every respect. In general, an individual is someone who can think, especially an entity with consciousness.

This definition is not random. Reading further you will realize that the distinct traits of these individuals are among the main reasons why they are likely to be *chosen*.

Below is a description of the targeted individuals by Brian Kofron, a former SIS agent who was part of the program to harass these people but chose to come out and defend them. "They are selected for many different reasons. Often because they are isolated. They don't have much money, friends or family. And they also tend to be very, very smart people. The aspects of this technology that they are interested in improving have to do with cognitive processes, with processing information. As a result, they want very smart people to be the targets of this program.

They also tend to target people who are involved in what I would call alternative research, commonly called conspiracy research, who disagree with the government, people who are researching things like 9/11. They're also interested in people who are involved in research about this technology. We have found that a high percentage of people who are targeted are people who are interested in or have information about very advanced technologies.

Usually these are related to directed energy, frequency weapons. Exactly the type of weapons that are discussed here and that are used in *voice to skull/synthetic telepathy induced by voice to skull technology*, and behavior modification, and many other aspects of this technology. Each individual fits the general profile I'm describing.

So, they are highly intelligent, and it is in their interest to be isolated by any means. They normally have a kind of what I would describe as a free mind. They are people who are not part of the crowd, so to speak, in the way they think.

You know? They're *the outsiders* (the black *lions* of society), they're what the government would call dissidents, or revolutionaries, or people who may be a problem.

Some TI-targeted *individuals* have said that this type of profile that all targeted individuals fall into is characterized by empowered individuals, and I would certainly agree with that. But I can't talk about how they actually identify such an individual. I think the general profile that I'm describing that fits the subjects of this program, is something that is generated at a high level within the program.

This is the federal government. We're talking at the highest levels of this social engineering program. We are scientists from across the country and around the world.

They look at:

-someone's genetics

-someone's cognitive abilities

-someone's genes

-someone's DNA

-people's social situation

-people's careers.

I was very surprised that so many PhD students are actually the targets of this program. They are usually PhD students who have gone against the mainstream of academia, of what academia normally teaches, usually in the fields of science and technology.

And the reason is that the people running the program want to cover certain technologies and certain aspects of science that can lead to extraordinary discoveries. These higher levels of science and technology are the exclusive purview of the classified branches of our government and military, and as a result, it follows that the American people have no right to this information and it is in the national security interest of our country to keep it classified.

But once these people are selected, they will have an entire tracking band (transmission frequency) of the *voice to skull/voice to skull* program running against them. This is detailed in my article at the *157 Roy Street* section of my website.

They will organize planned harassment and stalking campaigns, run career sabotage programs against them to ruin their jobs. They will have character assassination campaigns run against them in their neighborhood. They will be isolated from family and friends as these people are turned against them.

And they will be isolated slowly, slowly, over time, using the technology itself. Many people get scared, understandably, when they don't know what it is at first. Many times, they end up going to a psychiatrist and, false diagnoses of manic depressive schizophrenia, delusional delusions, delusional paranoia are written against these individuals and it turns out that it is a loophole in the law that is being used to take away people's constitutional rights.

Because once you are deemed mentally incompetent, i.e. unable to take care of yourself, i.e. depressed, delusional, paranoid, the state or federal government uses that as an excuse to come in and say they have to take care of you.

So, I warn all the targeted individuals, please do not [...] do not allow them to put a diagnosis against you, because this is a dirty trick that they are using to take away the rights of people across the country.

This is discussed very openly within the SIS and with some of the liaison contacts in the EESC[48], Amazon, as well as with members of the military who are in a civilian capacity. One thing you have to understand is that in the security field, most of the people who work there are ex-military and ex-intelligence people.

And many of them, in fact, are still active intelligence agents. And they've simply been reassigned to the internal service to work with a private security company, specifically for the purpose of running this highly illegal program that's being run against TIs/target individuals everywhere, so, target

---

[48] **The EESC** European Economic and Social Committee provides a forum for representatives of different economic and social groups to advise the European institutions on economic and social legislation.

individuals all the way, what I would call people who are under the total influence of voice to skull/voice to skull V2K technology.

[...] But one of the things that worries me is that the technology, as it is being researched and developed in Seattle, uses emotion manipulation and behavior manipulation, without the *harassment play* and without the V2K/voice-to-skull technology features.

Thus, this use of technology can be done very discreetly, to the point where the person against whom it is being used will not know that the technology is being used against them.

And this is one of my main concerns and one of the reasons why I want to bring more clarity to this technology and to this issue, because this technology could potentially be used against tens to hundreds of millions of Americans every day. I recognize that I've mentioned in some of my podcasts that there are field effects where this technology will not be directed at one person, but it will create a general field of frequency in a geographic area so that everyone in that geographic area will feel the effects of the technology. It is more a general application of the technology rather than an individual, specific application of the technology.

But if we consider that use and the fact that it's being used to alter emotions, thinking, and behavior, then we could be looking at many, many millions of people across the country who are under the influence of technology today, right now. So in that general field they can broadcast a frequency that affects the human beings in that frequency field and induce a general state of happiness or sadness, anger, agitation, tranquility, and in that way have a general effect on the city; I've seen this done and it's remarkable how effective it is, because if you walk down a street in Seattle, you'll see people in a bad mood, all at the same time and not knowing each other, and then you walk over a block or two to another office building and walk in and see exactly the same things happening there. It's very, very, very disturbing. So within that bubble or frequency zones everybody, is let's say in a bad mood.

They, (and under those circumstances), can still *inject* a frequency specific to the targeted individual, say, a homeless person in Seattle that they experience 24 hours a day.

So, they will be under the influence of the general state of agitation or bad mood that everyone else is in, and then under the influence of the specific frequency that is directed at them.

They can literally stop your own thoughts and replace them with other thoughts, sending thoughts into your head. And it's so sophisticated that you can't tell where these thoughts are coming from. There's no way to discern that they're coming from anywhere other than your own mind.

So, you can imagine how bad it would be for people who don't even realize this technology exists. And they have these thoughts that they think are spontaneous because they are under the influence of this technology.

And being on both sides of this technology, I am amazed/dismayed at how it works.

And I know that the thoughts that I'm putting into your head are coming from exactly the same place in your mind that your own natural thoughts come from. So, if I didn't know that I was under the influence of this technology, then I would have no idea that someone was influencing my thoughts. And that's exactly what it could be used for.

It could be used to influence people's opinion, to get them to agree with a certain agenda. It could be used to turn groups of people or individuals against each other for any purpose. This affects the most intimate part of the human being. It's a huge, huge problem. And you can imagine the applications of this if someone ever wanted to start a riot.

If anyone would ever want to increase the crime rate, and then of course you know you can use it for the exact opposite. You can use it to lower the crime rate by making everyone passive.

And that could have some bad applications. If you want people to be passive, not paying attention and not taking action, it could be used for that purpose as well.

So, yes, my mind boggles at the possibilities in terms of using this device." **Bryan Kofron-former SIS agent**

"Targeted individuals are those who face various forms of surveillance harassment. Almost all target individuals have experienced chronic, highly organized persecution. Many targets also experience the sudden and unexplained breakdown of personal and work relationships. Businesses are sabotaged and become unsustainable. Items in locked homes and cars usually disappear. Computers constantly malfunction and seem to be controlled from the outside, phones are hacked, cloned, and automobiles are in constant need of repair.

Then there are what appear to be electronic assault activities that affect both mind and body. Symptoms range from burning sensations on or in different parts of the body to hearing internal voices and uncontrolled movements of the arms and legs.

The result for those affected is a life without hope, a life characterized by unrelenting fear, resentment, pain and despair. In the United States, the military is credited with developing the technology to implement this *fantastic* campaign to destroy the human psyche, but that is not the whole story.

The reality is that targeting is by no means limited to being an *American* problem. Rather, it is a global one, and while few targets understand the real agenda behind the predatory attacks they suffer, the truth is that no target was chosen at random." Gaye Leto, *Who are the targeted individuals?*

In the opening of the book you could read about the technology and weapons that are being used to target these people.

They need agents, real people to help them implement their insidious agenda. The more of us who report this agenda, the more beneficial it is for our current situation and the future of our freedom and future generations. There would be empirical data on the symptoms from the testimonies of many people. They usually use this technology in different areas of the country and on different individuals, different profiles to make it seem random and isolated, and not to spot the pattern.

The answer to the question *Who are the target individuals?* differs depending on who is responding or rather the interests they serve.

"The FBI, CIA agents still in the system or those who know about the program want to keep it secret, or undercover.

They use active denial tactics.

They say the targets are mentally ill, delusional and schizophrenic. That they want attention, a road to fame or unwarranted compensation. Compensation for pain and suffering. And the whistleblowers who have gotten out of the system are according to them disgruntled intelligence agents, police officers or other forces who have been fired or highlighted and just want compensation from the department they worked for, and revenge.

Drug abuse is usually assumed or implied. Veterans who are targeted individuals suffer from PTSD and have dissociated from reality due to unhealed trauma from the war. Targeted individuals are suspected criminals."

Those who have come out of the system and are tortured day in and day out, just like the innocent people who go through a daily ordeal, will answer differently. These details will be mentioned by most law enforcement.

However, the target individuals are good people with extraordinary abilities, they have a good background, a mind of their own and cannot be manipulated, they are creative and have faith, they are beautiful in spirit.

The authors have deduced that this whole sinister system is based on the law of cause and effect, that the perpetrators of this machine put others to do the deeds in order to divert attention away from themselves.

The one, those who set this monster of a program in motion have behind them a belief of torture and much suffering, otherwise it cannot be explained. They most likely feed off of it, and most likely monetize off of the suffering of these innocent people. There is a constant line from beginning to end that follows this thread unnatural to man and God, it is unnatural in every way and very dark.

Target individuals have a high IQ, are intuitive, empathetic, artistic, compassionate, empowered, free thinkers and are very vocal.

In general, the target individuals seem to fall into specific groups where intelligence, soul, soulful beauty predominate as well as their free spirit. They are beings who do not follow order, and who like justice, they have order encoded in their genes, they do not need rules to tell them what is right or wrong. They just know. And they act like it. Do not be fooled by detractors masquerading as target individuals. It is an insidious practice by the same agents provocateurs. They have leadership skills that cannot be corrupted as they are interested in helping society prosper. These targets are usually identified at an early age.

They seem to be traumatized from early childhood and have traumatic events inserted into them in a staged and calculated manner to break their spirit, create multiple personalities and/or possibly for experimentation.

They are under constant but covert monitoring from an early age being programmed to become *a persona/mask,* which they can use on command when the time is right.

These people are believed to have diverse genes, and with the interventions of beneficial watchers, have managed to withstand the psychic torture.

They have a potential that many do not have and are often envied, marginalized, loved possessively and obsessively, used for their intelligence and the way they place information together, draw conclusions or ideal solutions. Everything is easier for them because, as a priest once said, "God hears some people faster".

Target people can be any individuals from all walks of life. They are destroyed in stages, to be *rebuilt* again, some would say. It starts by creating emotional problems to induce stress, confusion, distress.

In these cases, distress is induced or transferred to them by the methods already described. Emotional shock can come from traumatic break-ups, violence, or more serious reasons. There are many families that have been destroyed. And the targeted individuals know how many loved ones they have lost to be destabilized.

The concept of family and beauty is falling apart. Every known and unknown method is being tried, every online medium is being used to show how good it is to be *without these family responsibilities*, without a family. Of course they want you alone and isolated, and under constant monitoring so one does not elevate spiritually, because this way they found out the truth.

And for those who want a family, stability, not knowing that they are preys, detractors are put in their way by various agents sent temporarily to hurt them even more, use them, leave them eventually taking everything from them. It can be noted a sort of pride in doing evil and being proud of the evil done which Mengele spoke of, and which he wished to implement to form the satanic church, not to help spiritual fulfillment.

According to some sources, these programs vary depending on the trauma. That's why it's important to know yourself. Attempts will be made to insert subtle programs containing false personalities, from which you would believe that the new personalities belong to you. The ones used to feeling, noticing, will perceive the artificial change immediately. Why is it important not to accept these programs or input thoughts? In order not to weaken your connection with self, your lucidity and your connection with the Good God.

The target people are people who have or have had successful careers, families who loved them, friends and beautiful social circles.

Gradually they are isolated, *accidentally* meet people who steal from them, create all kinds of problems, slander them, separate them from their husbands and wives, children. All kinds of problems are created, they induce addictions in their loved ones, they induce all sorts of problems with their children, pets, and generally speaking destructive programs. Sometimes it's for the better, but it's how it happens that makes the difference.

If you are careful, you can quite easily repreprehend this *modus operand,i* and do something in advance. In the first place do not accept negative suggestions about yourself or flattery programs so as not to create addictions that feed on vanity, so that against a background of exacerbated vanity you do not make wrong decisions. Pay attention to suggestions and ask for a pause for thought if you sense something is amiss. Train your intuition and observe yourself. Make comparisons with what you have been and check for references about yourself so you know when a new acquired behavior is induced.

Obviously, these are personal opinions and experiences, you will apply what you think serves you or nothing. You are mature people with your own life experience, and there are many specialists who can offer you specialized services. Perhaps in the future we will describe in detail ways out of such situations.

Profile creation

If you have these symptoms, you have most likely been under observation for a long time. Why?

For the many reasons listed here or none at all. Some people leave the "wrong" people. The authors have found that there are groups that in exchange for money, will commit to destroying one's life, wholly or in part, depending on how much they get.

What kind of technology do you think they're using, and why isn't the government doing anything about it?

How do they find out about you? You talk on the phone. Everything is recorded, dated, written down. They know everything about you, your schedule, reactions, your thought pattern and response to stimuli, what you drink and eat, your vices and virtues in other words.

Targets will be observed long before they become aware that they are being watched. Profiles will be created by:

-the long-term and consistent *attention* and the people close to them

-breaking into targets' homes and searching through their personal belongings so as to leave traces (gradually inducing psychosis and paranoia)

- eavesdropping on phone conversations and hacking into laptops; attempts are made to obtain sensitive information about the person in question so that it can then be used against him/her in various contexts, from love affairs to the mundane affairs in traffic

-gathering information from friends and family

-watching your favorite places to eat, shop

-observing weaknesses (bribery, lying, the pleasure of money), displeasures

What can they blackmail, harass, scorn you with? How can you best be controlled?

You don't need to suspect everyone, unless you have cumulatively many signs that you are a target then you may want to consider the scenarios presented.

If you notice that relationship dynamics are gradually being destroyed by all sorts of negative coincidences, it would be good to analyze the new inserts in your lives even if they are not suspicious and especially if your thinking pattern has already changed.

That is, if there are any changes in your thought process regarding observations, level of attention to details, listening to your nervous system and intuition.

Once your profile is made, they start with the steps mentioned below:

1. Emotional shock: sudden breakups (because of false evidence, ideas in the mind that usually do not belong to the victims), sudden departures without a word, beatings, violence, theft, disasters, even calms, adultery, etc.

2. Isolation of the individual: everything that can mean isolating the individual whether in a couple or not.

In this case the individual is only allowed to go out at certain times, hours and occasions. If he tries to exercise his own free will he is stopped or set up so that he does not go "outside the word of the programmers".

They are made to feel melancholy, depression. There are repeatedly created false quarrels for trivial reasons in order to lose the support and friendship of their loved ones, and to create a lack which they then fill in by belonging to their groups. It is usually this group that manipulates him from the shadows for its own interests. A battle for the souls.

In general, they use technologies like voice to skull/V2K, forcing you to say things you don't want to say in order to escalate aggression, arguments, to make *it easier to* give up a situation, to violate your will. What they are aiming for is dehumanization.

3. Blatant stalking and harassment in different situations

4. Psychic torture which varies from case to case, and which starts from the phases of subtle observation: mild depressions alternating with exhilarating states, headaches, ruminations, unexpected fluctuations of *new* states and *personalities*, etc.

5. Breaking the spirit, breaking resistances and breaking the will, literally draining the life force, recording, capturing the electromagnetic activity of the brain (this is what they call the soul).

If the target individual accepts their proposal to be a pawn on their chess board, he is left alone, reconstructed. Suddenly the individual is "well", repaired and functional for the next steps. After stage 5 as a rule the individual has no will of his own, no faith, and his hope lies in the hands of these thieves of beauty and souls. But not all of them.

If you don't accept you will have repetitive attacks, but there are ways. They can only influence you through your mind, your habits, your detrimental circles. If you have a healthy circle with trustworthy people, stay grounded in that reality and love life.

These individuals despise life, divine beauty, family and usually revolve only around themselves. They want money, influence and power. Some don't have it is temporarily lent to them by those individuals who orchestrate and exploit weaknesses under the guise of liberation.

They're doing everything they can to get the victim to the wood chipper. But all is not lost. They are beneficent watchers, good people who help and genuinely care for the good of others. There are. Change your circles and band together. Seek help from trained people who are kind hearted. Unfortunately, even these specialists are persecuted and tried in every way in order to de-center them and steal their well-deserved laurels. Even so, your vigilance is stronger, your faith is greater, your soul is present and strong, the will to build a beautiful future belongs to you and is constant, the desire to live in the divine light and in God is greater than their subversive actions. Be firm, resolute and in your strength! They cannot stop you from living your life!

Even if they try to defeat you, you are stronger than you know and tougher than the mountains. Stand tall and fight for your souls!

The next steps differ depending on the individual

6.Turning the individual into a bait subject for others

7. Introducing the subject into political, economic, educational, social, etc. spaces.

It's a battle of the brains. If you resist *their temptation*, and the thoughts they induce, you can control them and get out from under their control. Mentally. Yes!!

It is an ancient method practiced by some and others who have altered the divine destinies for their personal pleasures, and have imposed their will on others, mocking the divine destiny. Live your life beautifully according to the divine plan!

They can't stop you. Unless you make *mistakes.* They assume themselves the rights *to punish* you by default. They falsely, call themselves lords of karma. There's no such thing. The judgment is God's alone! And this is no joke. There is a subsystem that does that, but they take it as a game inducing indescribable pain.

They may lure you into their guilds or groups of all kinds which can have a bad influence on you in the long run. But there are also those healthy groups that don't have the air of sects set up at the behest of *friends* overseas. There are also healthy, beautiful and balanced environments.

What will happen from now on will be total chaos but under invisible control from our point of view. Not that it isn't already.

In all the above stages, in order to gain control over you, they will go out of their way to induce: states of fear, paranoia, self-criticism and criticism of others, guilt for anything even for breathing, submissiveness, self-doubt, all to follow another opinion, perhaps *a master* who initiates you into his clique, or organization.

We apologize, but I cannot have respect for these mutineers. The true constructs, defenders of faith, virtues are we, the peaceful vocal individuals, the visionaries, the lovers of harmony and freedom, the helpers. But if we want peace, at times, we have to unfortunately prepare for war. Not because we wanted but because we are left with no option but defend ourselves.

They have parasitized the Earth with their cults and practices, initiations, false sovereignties and so-called beneficial ideologies from which they have also extracted benefits while leaving the common mortal to fight for a loaf of bread.

No! We can't agree to that. To believe in something that is not God's way.

We may be saying the wrong thing, but analyzing the injustices and saying things like "Maybe God has been preparing you all this time for what's coming." Really? Whose God is this?

God doesn't need to test us. He already knows us. I think someone else needs experiments to control God's creation.

My God is a good God, who does not believe in trauma for perfection but in education.

These monsters can even make some people feel guilty enough to commit regrettable acts. Keep faith and prayer close to the soul. They will induce false symptoms of possessions, which may "materialize," or images that represent fears you have. They hate life, and their acts prove it.

You will find yourself talking to yourself or arguing with a version of yourself in thought or some version of someone you know. There are robots programmed *to argue* with you, and highly advanced technologies that mimic or induce the described symptoms and voices of people you know. They need just 3 seconds of recording to mimic an entire conversation

And you, in broad daylight on the street, you want to argue about nothing. False jealousy, envy, admiration, love, sexual attraction. False because if you don't have any past history of such emotions, there's no way you can become envious or jealous overnight, unless is something induced somehow. For the point of sexual attraction, especially for ladies and young ladies, but also for gentlemen.

They will stimulate your nerves and the corresponding erogenous points in your brain to "feel attracted" to one of their envoys and to appear to feel natural. In a way they are responses generated as a result of stimulation, but they do not occur as a natural process unfolds, on the principle of soul affinit. Hence dissonance, dissociation, multipolarity, etc.

If you stay calm or let a few minutes pass, or simply excuse yourself and walk away from the situation, or give yourself a little time to determine if you have a trigger point, if it was a natural stimulus, the *symptoms* should go away.

You use sexual energy for creative actions that benefit you. It is an intense sensation mimicking a form of mystical ecstasy that is unhealthy and unnatural; it is not a consequence of natural attraction. Programs of love, affection, pleasure and so on are induced.

No, not all cases are like this, but in most cases yes, it is so. This does not mean that the affinity between souls does not exist or that love is a program. On the contrary!

According to our observations there has been much attempt to replace genuine love by stimulating certain centers to induce a loving, tingling sensation in the chest area. The difference is that some radiate similar to wave-like vibrations, whereas real love feels intense, total and gives an overall feeling of well-being.

They are emotions, different perceptions. Of course, everyone knows what they feel, the important thing is to determine the authenticity of your emotions and whether they belong to you.

We believe that the last stage, even though it could not be, is total dehumanization. Lack of sensitivity, care, a stage where feelings and intuition are targeted most.

π

Methods of harassment and persecution

These methods can be found on the OHCHR website[49] Office of the High Commissioner for Human Rights. They have been reported by numerous targeted individuals around the world. So, the methods these individuals use include, but are not limited to, the methods below.

1. **Surveillance** - stalking, electronic surveillance, computer and phone hacking, monitoring all online activities and bugging the home

2. **Victim profiling** is done to identify any weaknesses and insecurities for later use. Information often obtained through sexual partners or trusted people in their lives.

3. **Conditioning in which victims are sensitized to certain stimuli**, such as everywhere you go, someone will cough when they walk by. The goal is to become a cop on your own, only to later believe that anyone who coughs is engaging in harassment. People report that conditioning includes hand gestures, an overt use of color in people's clothing (like everyone you see wearing red) or cars of a

49
https://www.ohchr.org/sites/default/files/Documents/Issues/Torture/Call/Individuals/Harrassmenttechniques.pdf

certain color or with their headlights on (also known as brightness).

4. **Anchoring-** forced **isolation** usually achieved by frequent harassment, where someone will offer false arguments for harassment. Often, many possible arguments are put forth to keep the victim confused and cause them to focus on cycles of harassment from one possible reason to another, to keep the victim perpetually guessing and on their own, in each scenario the victim is at fault and causing self-doubt, fear to intimidation, and ultimately a destructive thought cycle.

5. **Mobbing** (group harassment in the workplace), where wherever the victim goes, they will have a large number of people or a number of people following them and will often use *key* words that the victim has been conditioned or the victim's name to get their attention.

6. **Street theater** in which a group will "perform" an overt activity, such as a mock confrontation or scenarios designed to test your reactions. It often takes the form of a couple who position themselves next to you and then carry on a conversation using many of your conditioned words or relating to your particular situation and sensitivities.

7. **The use of directional devices** that have the ability to direct sound to a single person in a crowded room. This particular item is ultimately the most commonly used and is often referred to as V2K/Voice to Skull and is widely used in psychological victim restraint.

Initially, Voice to skull technology is used to cause the victim to doubt their own mental health, and lead to hospitalization in a mental health system, and later just to torture them and   never give the victim a moment of privacy or peace. If she enters the mental health system, then the stalking increases dramatically because the victim has now been *discredited* and can be labeled as someone with a mental problem if she talks about stalking or thought-inducing technology in the mind by stimulating points in the skull.

Also in this context is tracing, a method whereby artificial intelligence analyzes sounds and the environment around you in order to manipulate the way you hear and perceive the sounds around you.

8. **The use of electronics to impair vision and balance**, which was originally developed for military and police use in crowd control called *dazzling/vision-taking* that can make you vomit.

9. **Campaigns, sound raids** which are a technique of harassment of the individual in the community in which abnormal sound levels are directed at the victim and the victim's home.

These include:

-cars that deliberately break or accelerate as they pass,

-people who talk excessively loudly at all hours of the night,

-amplification of sound using directional speakers so that external sounds that were previously inaudible can now be heard,

-trucks of garbage and other heavy vehicles and countless other deliberate tactics.

10. **Sleep deprivation** - this is perhaps one of the most insidious tactics used where victims are woken up several times a night and can be kept awake for days. The effects are dramatic and completely debilitating, affecting concentration, mood, irritability, physical appearance, mental health and have a significant impact on all areas of their life - job performance, relationships, and significantly damage the victim's image to the point of discredit as they appear disorganized, disordered. Thus sleep patterns are altered so that they can sleep during the day (when noise campaigns are more effective) and be awake at night

(where they can be portrayed as the noise-maker and a disruptive member of the community).

11. **Luring or entrapment** where, victims are harassed to the point where they attack and commit a crime, such as assault, breaking and entering or vandalism, while trying to locate the source of the harassment. Stalkers will actively try to provoke verbal and physical confrontations especially after a period of sleep deprivation.

Or victims are pushed into an activity that can later be used as blackmail. The activities can be business, sexual, drug or other criminal activities.

12. **Gaslighting/Manipulation by Psychological Abuse**, which is a form of psychological abuse in which someone will actively try to undermine the victims and make them doubt themselves so that they lose all their self-confidence and self-esteem and are therefore more easily manipulated and pushed down the path of questioning their mental health.

It can be as simple as victims being told something that the perpetrators later deny. They also call the victims *stupid* only for the situation to be turned into an attack on the person. It can be incredibly effective coming from a trusted person and before the victim understands what is happening to them. So, denying a true fact and then accusing that the true fact never happened, inducing psychosis, paranoia or distrust of their own person.

13. **Blackops jobs/Clandestine** or undercover **operations** to infiltrate various structures in order to obtain information.

In context it is a term where a stalker enters a victim's property and deliberately places something or deliberately moves something. The purpose is to cause self-doubt and fear that their property is being accessed, which victims then try to sell as a result.

14. **Propaganda and misinformation** is also the other key element to suppress knowledge of this practice, as its effectiveness initially requires that the victim is initially unaware of the existence of gang stalking, psychological abuse through manipulation of reality or electronic technologies such as directional speakers. Thus huge amounts of online time are devoted to creating misinformation sites that attempt to discredit victims by promoting the mental health agenda.

They do this by posing as victims and actively trying to make themselves look crazy so that all victims are treated as victims. Also by setting up websites claiming to help victims and to be a resource for victims to come together and then harassing them to the extent that they lose hope and stop seeking help, causing further isolation.

15. In addition to the above, **gang stalkers/aggressors rely on mistrust and disparagement** and, as such, much of the bullying is designed (at least initially) **to mimic mental health problems**. They also rely on their abuse being so extreme, so pervasive, so fundamentally immoral as to be unbelievable. So victims then resort to photographing, videotaping and recording their daily encounters to refute with evidence the countless unsubstantiated allegations made against them - in particular in relation to denying what the gang stalkers are saying or events they are trying to deny and trying to induce paranoia or irrationality in victims. Victims are made to feel helpless because any attempt to defend themselves is used against them and, when they do seek help, they are met with distrust or open hostility.[50]

The above represent external actions that are carried out by various agents who may be ordinary people. Some are paid

---

50

https://www.ohchr.org/sites/default/files/Documents/Issues/Torture/Call/Individuals/Harrassmenttechniques.pdf so are consciously involved in these situations, others are blindly used according to a pre-determined program triggered on command. In either case, the soul dominates any programming.

*

Symptoms[51]

The symptoms that target individuals exhibit have been demonstrated through existing and patented technological breakthroughs. Below will be presented symptoms and related studies, devices. The evidence is older and newer. The purpose of mentioning them is to emphasize that they have been known about for a very long time, so they are not topical. The new findings are the stuff of science fantasy to some.

1. Hearing sounds, voices transmitted via microwaves
2. Transmission of specific commands to the subconscious mind

---

[51] All rights to the symptoms section belong to Mind Justice. For the original material please visit their website
https://www.mindjustice.org/#8 ,

3. Visual disturbances, visual hallucinations
4. Injecting words, numbers into the brain via electromagnetic radiation waves
5. Manipulating emotions
6. Remote mind reading
7. Pain provocation in any nerve in the body.
8. Remote manipulation of human behavior from space
9. Bullying, stress symptoms like helicopters flying overhead
10. The camera-like view through your eyes
11. Control sleep patterns
12. Computer-to-brain interface, control and communication
13. Complex brain control, such as retrieving memories, implanting personalities

To read the details of each symptom please visit the Mind Justice website[51]. We have been blocked numerous times when trying to access it

*

Below is the response I received after an e-mail was sent to an state institution that I asked to declassify, confirm or/and deny the existence of such a program, and whether it would be conducted on Romanian territory or cross-border and the immediate cessation of non-consensual use on the population. The original paper is image on the next page. The reply is translated down below.

Translation-petition addressed to the Romania Secret Services

"Following your petition addressed to the Romanian Secret Services and registered with the number 316322, from 13.02.2025, we bring you to your attention that the presented aspects have been analyzed with all availability but these (the presented aspects), exceed the legal competencies entrusted to our institution by the law nr. 51/1991 concerning the national security of Romania, republished with its modifications and subsequent completions, and the law no.14/1992 concerning the organization and functionality of the Romanian Secret Services, with its ulterior modifications and completions.

We thank you for your trust, reassuring you of the special care we hold for respecting the legality of our actions.

With esteem, The Chief of Public Relation Services"

Doamnei

Ca urmare a petiției dumneavoastră adresată Serviciului Român de Informații și înregistrată sub nr. 316/322 din 13.02.2025, vă aducem la cunoștință faptul că aspectele prezentate au fost analizate cu toată disponibilitatea, însă acestea excedează competențelor legale conferite instituției noastre prin Legea nr. 51/1991 privind securitatea națională a României, republicată, cu modificările și completările ulterioare și Legea nr. 14/1992 privind organizarea și funcționarea Serviciului Român de Informații, cu modificările și completările ulterioare.

Vă mulțumim pentru încrederea manifestată, asigurându-vă de grija deosebită ce o purtăm pentru respectarea legalității acțiunilor noastre.

Cu stimă,

Șeful Serviciului Relații cu Publicul

SERVICIUL ROMÂN DE INFORMAȚII
B-dul. Libertății nr. 14, Sector 5, 050706 - București - România; www.sri.ro

1 / 1

Below we have attached some of the studies we have found on the effects that radiation has on the human body, so when we have a surplus of electricity and more.

1. Microwave *radiation and* **health**: *A review of the literature (2001),* Author: S. R. H. Hall

This study reviews the available literature on the health effects of electromagnetic radiation, particularly microwaves. The author notes that non-ionizing radiation, such as that emitted by microwave communication satellites, does not cause direct DNA damage, but there may be a link between long-term exposure and *human health risks, such as changes to the central nervous system, cancer risks and possible sleep disturbances.*

2. Study on the effects of electromagnetic radiation on the blood-brain **barrier/Effects** *of electromagnetic fields on the blood-brain barrier* (2009), Author: R. D. Salford et al.

This study investigated the effects of electromagnetic fields on the blood-brain barrier and found evidence that microwave exposure can lead to changes in this barrier, which could lead to toxic substances entering the brain.

Although the study was carried out on animals, the research suggests that similar effects could occur in humans, especially with constant exposure to electromagnetic radiation.

3. Effects of *electromagnetic fields* **on sleep and** cognitive **function/Effects** *of electromagnetic fields on sleep and cognitive function* (2011), Author: F. Loughran et al.

This study analyzed the effects of electromagnetic fields, including microwaves, on sleep and cognitive function. The authors found that exposure to electromagnetic fields can *disrupt the sleep cycle, causing insomnia and reduced sleep quality.* These effects are particularly observed in cases of prolonged and intense exposure.

4.Psychological and physiological effects of electromagnetic fields in the workplace *Psychological and physiological effects of electromagnetic fields in the workplace* (2013), Author: A. A. S. Sadeghi et al.

This study investigated the effects of electromagnetic fields on the psychological and physiological state of workers constantly exposed to these radiations, including workers using satellite communication equipment. The study reported symptoms such as *mental fatigue, anxiety, irritability, irritability and difficulty concentrating, all associated with exposure to microwave and radio electromagnetic fields.*

5. *Effects of radiofrequency electro-***magnetic fields on reproductive health** (2012), Author: L. M. Rezk et al.

The study examines the effects of radio frequencies (also used in satellite communications) on reproductive health. *It suggested that long-term exposure to electromagnetic radiation can have a negative impact on fertility, in particular by lowering sperm counts and damaging sperm DNA structure.*

6. Electromagnetic **fields and human fertility***: A review of current research* (2014), Author: A. I. Kesari et al.

This study reviews research on the link between electromagnetic radiation (including microwaves and radio waves) and human fertility. The authors observed a correlation *between exposure to electromagnetic fields and decreased fertility, particularly in men, by reducing sperm quality.*

7. Long-term *exposure to radiofrequency electromagnetic fields and health risks* (2016), Author: R. A. Hardell et al.

This study examines the health risks associated with long-term exposure to electromagnetic fields, in particular microwave and radio radiation, and suggests a possible link between prolonged exposure and the risk of cancer, in particular brain cancer. The study refers to possible risks associated with exposure to microwave radiation emitted by satellites and other communication sources.

8. Study on radiofrequency radiation exposure and risk of glioma/Exposure *to radiofrequency radiation and risk of glioma: A case-control study* (2018), Author: M. S. Besson et al.

This study looked at the link between exposure to electromagnetic radiation and the risk of glioma (a type of brain cancer). Although they did not find direct and conclusive evidence, the authors emphasized the need for further studies to establish a clear correlation between microwave exposure and brain cancer risk.

9. Studies on the effects on the central nervous system/Effects *of electromagnetic fields on brain activity and sleep in humans* (2015), Author: D. L. Liboff et al.

This study investigates the effects of electromagnetic fields on brain activity and sleep in humans. A correlation has been found between exposure to electromagnetic fields (including those emitted by satellites) and altered brain waves, which can lead to sleep disturbances and decreased cognitive performance.

Maybe it will continue

_____